PRAISE FOR AUTOMATIC AUTHORITY

"Tarryn Reeves has struck gold in terms of what she has created in her book "Automatic Authority". There's a whole lot of fluff on how to market a service-based business online, but this book cuts straight to the point and tells you exactly what you need to do, to stand out, and become the go-to authority in your industry. If you're looking for a timeless playbook on how to simplify your marketing and rake in leads on autopilot, this is the book for you!"

- DIMITRI ROSS

"As a business owner, this is pure gold! Tarryn is so thorough in how she explains everything, and provides so much value in every step of the process from making the decision to write a book to becoming a bestseller. If you're even considering writing a book, you NEED to read this book!"

- KATIE POTRATZ

"This is an amazing resource for those looking to write their own book and really understand how to craft it in a way to maximize it being used for marketing. I love how straight forward this book is. Every chapter is concise and full of knowledge and what steps need to be taken."

- COLLEEN REAGAN

Automatic Authority

How to write a bestselling book that positions you as *THE* go-to authority in your industry, while simplifying your marketing and delivering a constant supply of loyal fans eager to buy your stuff

TARRYN REEVES

Published by Automatic Authority Publishing & Press House, Newcastle, NSW, Australia.

Tel: +61 417 785 921

www.automaticauthority.com

First published in Australia in 2024

The information in this book is the author's opinion only. Readers should not rely on the general information as a substitute for professional advice. The author and publisher cannot accept responsibility for any losses, damages or adverse effects that may result from using the information in this book.

A catalogue record for this book is available from the National Library of Australia.

ISBN: 978-0-6458469-8-0

To the courageous people who choose to step outside the box, build businesses and make an impact with their words. I see you. Keep going. You've got this.

CONTENTS

Section 3
WRITING YOUR BOOK

Section 4
PUBLISHING PATHWAYS

Section 5
LAUNCH AND MARKETING MASTERY

CONCLUSION

BONUS CONTENT

INTRODUCTION

In today's digital age, where content is king and the market is saturated with countless voices clamouring for attention, standing out as an authority in your field is not just an advantage, it's a necessity.

Automatic Authority is your comprehensive guide to crafting a non-fiction book that not only establishes you as the go-to expert, but also significantly amplifies your marketing efforts, attracting a steady stream of pre-qualified leads ready to engage in your business.

I don't know about you, but I think that's pretty darn cool. I am not interested in the hustle-hard culture. I tried it. For years, I struggled to fit into the suffocating box of conformity and the outdated notions of what a successful person looks like and how to achieve success as an entrepreneur.

That earned me a spectacular breakdown at the age of 23 and way more grey hair than should be peppering my head at the age of 36. So, I say 'Nope'. No #hustleandgrind for me, thank you very much!

As the mother of an eight-year-old girl and a newborn son, with a seemingly endless parade of hats to wear – as friend, CEO, counsellor, medic, referee, cleaner, cook, gardener, taxi driver, cheerleader, book midwife, chaos coordinator, dog mum, thought leader, speaker, author, human empowerment advocate, sustainable living enthusiast and book lover, to name but a few – I feel I have enough on my plate. I know you do, too.

I don't want to reach the end of my life feeling burnt out, uninspired and as if I just ran a marathon but with nothing to show for it. I want to slide on into my hundreds, looking slightly unhinged with my curls flying free, laughter lines crinkling the corners of my eyes and at the head of a freight train of memories filled with laughter, love and the knowledge that

I made a difference in the world. That's living done right, don't you think?

It is possible to stop hustling for clients, outshine your competitors, and be an industry-leading authority while still having time to do all the things you also want to do outside of how you make money.

Don't get me wrong. As a recovering workaholic and someone who absolutely adores my business, my clients and my team, I would, if left unsupervised and ignorant to the abundance of magic that exists outside the realm of my career, work all day every day. But we both know that there is more to life, right?

Can we do it all?

Can we really have it all?

Fuck yes, we can!

As savvy entrepreneurs, we also know that the digital landscape is crowded, and consumers are constantly bombarded with messages from countless sources. (I swear to God, if my phone dings again today with another spammy inbox message, I will throw the device into space!)

So, how can you rise above the noise and truly distinguish yourself as an expert in your field? The answer lies in the power of the written word, a timeless and enduring transformational portal that has the capacity to captivate, educate and inspire.

Many people aspire to writing a book, but it is an endeavour that few accomplish. The reasons are myriad: lack of time, unclear processes, fear of inadequacy or simply not knowing where to start.

Automatic Authority dispels these doubts, offering a clear, **actionable roadmap to start and complete your book within 28 days.** This isn't just about writing any book – it's about **creating a powerful tool that integrates seamlessly with your marketing strategy and enhances your brand's visibility, credibility and influence**.

This book is structured to walk you through every stage of the process, from honing your unique idea that resonates with your target audience to researching, writing, publishing and marketing your book. Each chapter is designed to build upon the last, creating a comprehensive framework that any entrepreneur can follow, regardless of previous writing experience.

In these pages, you will discover why crafting a book is not just a creative endeavour, but the fastest route to becoming the go-to authority in your niche. We will unravel the underlying principles and psychology behind this method, revealing why it is an unparalleled tool for establishing your expertise and attracting a steady stream of eager leads while you sip mojitos on the beaches of Bali or read your little ones a bedtime story.

You will start by laying the foundation – identifying your unique voice and the message that you want to share with the world. Understanding your audience is crucial, and *Automatic Authority* will guide you through conducting effective market research to ensure your book exceeds the expectations of your ideal readers.

The journey continues with actionable advice on structuring your book, establishing productive writing habits and creating content that engages and persuades. You'll learn how to overcome common obstacles writers face, such as writer's block and time management challenges, ensuring a smooth and efficient writing process.

Design, formatting and editing are also covered in detail, ensuring your book is professional and polished, reflecting the quality of the message you're sharing. With the myriad of publishing options available today, *Automatic Authority* will help you navigate the pros and cons of traditional versus hybrid publishing versus self-publishing, guiding you to make the best decision for your book and business.

But writing and publishing your book is just the beginning. The comprehensive marketing strategies provided will ensure your book reaches your intended audience: generating buzz, building anticipation and securing your position as an authority in your field.

Automatic Authority is more than just a book – it's a catalyst for transformation. It's designed not only to guide you in your writing, but also to elevate your brand, expand your influence and grow your business.

By the end of this book, you will not only have a clear blueprint for writing and publishing yours within 90 days, but also a strategic tool that enhances your marketing efforts, positions you as an authority in your field and generates a flood of pre-qualified leads ready to buy what you're selling.

Preferring to practice before I preach, I have done all and more of what I am sharing within these pages. I am a bestselling author of multiple books, a freelance writer and a public speaker. I have worked with hundreds of clients worldwide to get their messages seen and heard by their desired audience. I want to do the same with you. Whether you buy my courses, work with my team and me on a more intimate basis or simply action what you learn through reading this book, the one you write will change your business, your life and who you are as a person in all the juiciest ways.

My clients and I have used this method to simplify our marketing, to deliver our businesses a steady flow of clients and opportunities on autopilot, and to add a star-like influence to our names on a global scale. For most of us, the level of influence we have achieved comes second to the impact we make. But whatever your flavour, I've got you covered.

This book is more than just words on paper. It's a comprehensive resource that provides practical templates, invaluable resources and proven techniques that will empower you to craft a book that not only educates but also captivates and converts.

Want to know the best part? It's way easier and more fun than you think. Plus, you can have this project done as fast as your heart desires. It took me seven days – broken into two segments – to write this book. The first draft was done when I was 34 weeks pregnant and then finalised as I held my new son, Harvey, in my arms. Literally. If I can do it, so can you.

Now, let's go together on this adventure to authorship, authority and business growth. **By the time you turn the final page, not only will you have unlocked the secrets of authoritative writing you will also be well on your way to establishing yourself as a leader in your field, simplifying your marketing and flipping a farewell forever bird to the hustle and grind of outdated notions of entrepreneurship.**

Your audience is waiting. Your expertise is needed. So, strap in, stock up on gummy bears (Haribo is my brand of choice), and get ready to learn and then to do. And let's have some fun **turning you into the most sought-after and respected person in your field.**

SECTION 1

THE POWER OF AUTHORSHIP FOR YOUR AUTHORITY

CHAPTER 1

HUSTLE CAN HUSTLE ON OUTTA HERE

Let me tell you about a young woman named Harriet.

In the bustling heart of a port city, amid the relentless symphony of car horns and hurried footsteps, Harriet embodied the spirit of hustle. Day and night, weekends and holidays, she toiled tirelessly, chasing success with an unwavering determination that seemed to defy human limits.

Harriet had been moulded from a young age to believe that hard work was the only path to prosperity. The path to a successful life was, in very clear terms, laid out for her, and she was expected to follow it lest she disappoint somebody or end up on the streets: unmarried, unsuccessful and a disgrace to the modern world.

That she would go to university was never in doubt, and she was expected to choose from a list of acceptable degrees in which to graduate.

Harriet chose to study radiation therapy despite having no interest at all in working in a hospital. She just wanted to help people and make those around her proud. Two years into her degree with only a few months until graduation, Harriet couldn't take it anymore. After doing a work placement at a children's hospital in Sydney and seeing so many young people desperately sick and dying, her heart hurt too much. She knew she had to make a change.

Despite intense feelings of failure, shame and guilt for letting her family down, Harriet chose to study criminology at a different university.

To counteract her feelings of failure, she decided to do the degree via distance education and work full time for a railway company, doing 12-hour shifts on a day/night roster. Overachievement became the antidote and mask she used to hide the fact that she really wasn't all that interested in the traditional path to success anyway (although this conscious awareness came much later).

As Harriet made her way through her criminology degree, she also threw herself headlong into climbing the corporate ladder. Her days were spent in a relentless frenzy, constantly seeking opportunities, networking with influential people, and burning the midnight oil to ensure she never let anyone down and that she would 'be successful'.

At 23, Harriet was earning six figures, driving a new car, wearing suits, toting a laptop bag, catching the train to work, and sitting in a corner office overlooking the harbour. She had just bought her first home.

Her friends admired her dedication, and many looked up to her as a role model. But deep down, Harriet harboured a secret. She was trapped in a never-ending cycle of hustling. She was desperately unhappy.

As years passed, Harriet's health deteriorated. She had no time for proper meals and never got a restful night's sleep. She also exercised hard in order to keep herself looking how society told her she must as a young woman – fit, healthy and slim. Her relationships with friends, family and herself suffered as she prioritised work above all else. Stress and anxiety became constant companions. The sparkle in her eyes had long since faded, replaced with shingles along her spine and a mysterious rash along her jaw that nobody could seem to diagnose.

Harriet ended up on the not-so-comfy sofa of a counsellor, who was contracted to provide a service for company employees. He pointed out how unhappy she was and suggested that maybe she should look for a less stressful career. Harriet, being the overachiever that she was and believing that any sort of inability to perform at the highest level at all times was a sign of weakness, walked out of his office and didn't go back.

A year or so later, Harriet had started hallucinating and lucid dreaming, and her physical health had continued to deteriorate. Her family and new husband dragged her to see her doctor. The doctor gently informed Harriet that she had post-traumatic stress disorder (PTSD), chronic anxiety and major depression. Harriet burst into hysterical tears, angrily yelling that there was no such thing and that she was absolutely fine, just a little tired.

The doctor calmly and kindly explained that she was indeed suffering from this trifecta of stress-induced trauma and told her she should consider going on anti-depressants. After much back-and-forth, Harriet agreed to try the pills.

The medication took the edge off, and Harriet quit her high-flying career overnight with no plan B. She did some temp work here and there before eventually landing a position doing the rosters for a not-for-profit organisation. Only a few months into the job, the company went through a restructuring. The week she was due to go on a five-week vacation to the UK, Harriet was told she was being made redundant, effective immediately.

That's okay, she thought. *I'll go on this holiday and get another job when I get back.* While away, Harriet found out she was pregnant. On her return to Australia, she applied for numerous jobs, always disclosing that she was pregnant and expecting a baby in a few months. She did not want to 'lie' to her potential employers: the people-pleaser is always hard to kill off.

Unsurprisingly, Harriet found it difficult to get a job. So, she decided to enjoy her pregnancy and find paid work after her baby was born. She struggled with not having her days filled with traditional work deadlines but distracted herself with preparations for the baby's arrival. Only six weeks after her daughter's birth, new mum Harriet realised she really wasn't cut out for this stay-at-home mum gig and needed to get back to work as soon as possible.

She happened upon a post in a Facebook group – an entrepreneur was looking for someone to help with some administrative work. The short and flexible hours would 'suit a stay-at-home mum'. Harriet applied and got the job. Thus began her accidental entrepreneurial career.

As she worked to start and grow her business, many of Harriet's old habits came back in full force. Further feeding these habits was the toxic world of hustle entrepreneurship. Instagram was awash with hashtags like #girlboss, #hustleharder and #bossbabe, accompanied by images of women who seemed to be doing effortlessly what Harriet was trying to do, and managing to look like goddesses as they did it.

Ideas like "needing to create social media content and post it to every platform conceivable at least three times a day otherwise you would fail" were popular at the time. The baseline vibe was …

YOU WILL FAIL unless you:

- ✓ Have the sexiest brand.
- ✓ Create an inhuman amount of social media content and post at least three items a day to every platform at exactly the right time, even on weekends or while on holiday.
- ✓ Keep growing your email list.
- ✓ Send at least one email to that list per week.
- ✓ Feature a fantastic website.
- ✓ Offer interesting business cards.
- ✓ Have the perfect value ladder.
- ✓ Have the fanciest customer relationship management (CRM) system.
- ✓ Employ the best sales team.
- ✓ Have a calendar filled with Zoom calls.

And on and on it went.

Harriet did it all. Yet no matter how many hours a day she worked, how hard she hustled, she ended up exhausted and resentful that she couldn't achieve the seven-figure business that the coaches promised, or the four-hour work week that was alluded to and the #laptoplifestyle and freedom she dreamed of.

Yes, her business grew. Yes, she made money. Yes, she was passionate about what she did, and it sure beat her corporate career.

But at what cost?

She was working longer hours than ever and for way less money. She was on the fast track to burnout for the second time.

Yes, you probably guessed it by now – Harriet was me. And I know you can recognise pieces of yourself and/or your own journey in my story.

I was sick of taking Zoom calls with people only to find they had no cash to invest but just wanted to 'pick my brain' or, worse still, that they didn't even deem the call important enough to show up for it.

I'm an introvert and a Projector (for those of you who are into Human Design). I am not designed to talk to people all day. I loathe it. Don't get me wrong. I like people, but in very small doses. I need to retreat to my cave of solitude and fill my cup before returning to the human process of 'peopling' again. This is why I have a whole career developed around books dammit! I don't want to sit on calls all day every day.

And don't even get me started on emails. If any email looks even slightly like it's not written personally to me, I just delete it. If I need a product or service, I will go out and seek it from the people who have done a good job in showing me why they are the person I should buy from – usually in the form of a podcast, a heartfelt social media post or, better yet, a book.

So why did I think that pushing myself to send a boring email to my list every week would yield results? Because that is what I was told a successful businessperson does, and I believed it. For a while at least.

My whole life I had been told that the path to a successful life was:

Step 1: Go to school and get good grades.

Step 2: Go to university, get good grades and graduate with a degree that would give access to a socially desirable career path.

Step 3: Get a job in a socially desirable career that pays a lot of money, and climb the corporate ladder.

Step 4: Meet a man who could 'look after' me and whom everyone deemed 'acceptable'.

Step 5: Get engaged to said man.

Step 6: Get married and invite everyone you know and who your family wants to have there, even if it's not what you want.

Step 7: Buy a nice house in a nice neighbourhood.

Step 8: Have a baby.

Step 9: Have another baby.

Step 10: Continue to work your 9 to 5 job while looking like a woman out of the pages of a magazine, nurturing your children, keeping the house in showroom condition, and smiling – goddamit – while you do it all.

Step 11: Continue until you are at least 65.

Step 12: Retire.

Step 13: Die.

What kind of madness is that? Even though I subscribed to this "13 Step to Life Success" philosophy for a good 20 years or so, the entire time something inside me was screaming: *I didn't sign up for this! There must be more! Where are the soul-deep conversations that create genuine human connections? Where are the adventures that make you smile every time you think about them years later? Why would I want to wake up and feel anything less than in love with the life I'm living?*

I'm also a realist and I'm not saying everything needs to be happy and glittery rainbows all the time. I'm a big fan of feeling all the feelings, whatever those may be – happiness, anger, joy, grief, pain. Feelings are how we know we are alive and are part of the human experience.

What I am saying is, for those of us who remember, we have a choice – we can choose differently. We can create a life and a business that allows us to live life on our terms – one where we can choose how to spend each minute of the precious time given to us here on Earth. The book you write will free up your time and allow you to sell to serious prospects who are ready to buy.

Some days we will need to work harder than others. Some days we will feel like throwing in the towel and questioning why we ever wanted to start a business in the first place. Some days we will find so much joy in the freedom and expansion of doing exactly what it is we came here to do. And it's all beautiful.

So, if you are the type of entrepreneur who, like me, is completely uninterested in subscribing to the culture of "hustle hard or die trying", then this book is for you.

A pivotal moment for me came when I discovered (or rather remembered) the power of storytelling. I'm not talking about the imaginary world of fictional stories. I'm talking about the non-fiction kind. The real, raw, messy, chaotic, vulnerable, authentic side of storytelling. The kind that has the power to move people, change lives and transform worlds. This is the kind of storytelling that I insist we all get courageous enough to share, because this is where the genuine magic happens.

It doesn't even have to go as deep and personal as I have with my story. Instead, you can stick to teaching others what you know, sharing your wisdom and allowing others to learn from you (don't be so damn selfish in keeping all that learning to yourself). Telling stories is how we learn, connect and grow. It's a system of connection that has stood the test of time and I know this to be true – stories will never die. They are part of what makes us human.

There are many platforms from which to tell your story and share what you know, and I say use them all. A book, however, is undoubtedly the most impactful.

The power of a book for entrepreneurs

For hundreds of years, savvy entrepreneurs, such as Alex Hormozi, Gabrielle Bernstein, Russell Brunson, Sophia Amoruso, Tony Robbins, Carrie Green and Sabri Suby, have used books as a sales tool that effortlessly allows them to scale their businesses, build trust, generate authority and fill their pipelines with prospects already pre-qualified to buy. They've done this without getting on a single sales call or wasting hours they would rather spend on anything other than another soul-sucking webinar or nipple-drying sales call.

Just to be clear, you may still choose to jump on the occasional sales call, but those will be with people who already feel like they know you, are excited to learn from you, and may just have a few qualifying questions. Those calls hit differently. More of those, please.

Even better, the more people who read your book (and there will be many because you have your act together and are going to market this thing once it's written), the more money you will make. You can literally screw up every other part of your marketing but your book – which you wrote once, set up and set free – will continue to bring you a reliable, steady source of pre-qualified, ready-to-buy aligned clients on autopilot.

Here's why a book is the best method for entrepreneurs to convey their stories and connect with their audience.

Efficiency and cost-effectiveness

Traditional methods of client acquisition often involve high costs and significant friction. Imagine trying to introduce yourself to potential clients through a typical sales funnel (I bet you've been there!). You might start with a video sales letter or training, hoping to capture interest. This is followed by a call to action, usually one urging viewers to book a call. Here's where the friction begins: potential clients must invest time to watch your video, muster the courage to book a call, and brace themselves for a possible hard sell on the other end. This process is laden with resistance and opportunities for potential clients to drop off.

In contrast, a book provides a low-friction entry point. Priced between $3 and $17, a book is affordable for most people. This low cost means the financial risk for the reader is minimal. If they don't enjoy the book, the loss is insignificant. This affordability and low risk lower the barriers to entry, making it easier for you to capture the interest of potential clients.

Building trust and reciprocity

When someone purchases your book, they invest money and time to understand your story, insights, and expertise. As they read, they build a relationship with you. Through the pages, you offer value, insights, and a piece of yourself, fostering a sense of reciprocity. The reader feels they are getting to know you, creating a bond that is far more personal and impactful than any video sales letter.

Immediate transformation and engagement

A book offers an immediate opportunity for transformation. As readers consume your content, they begin to experience shifts in their thinking, gain new perspectives, and see the potential for their own journeys. This immediate engagement is powerful. Unlike a sales funnel that requires multiple steps and significant commitment, a book lets readers experience your value proposition immediately. Without any pressure, they can decide if they want to take the next step with you.

A book is an efficient, cost-effective, and impactful way to introduce yourself to new clients, build trust and provide immediate value. A book paves the way for deeper connections and long-term relationships by reducing friction and resistance.

When you write a good book (and you will because I am going to show you exactly how to do that), it will generate leads and sales, and inject profit into your business in a way that will have you scratching your head and wondering why you didn't think to do this sooner.

A book is a sales tool that will allow your business to scale with ease. The book you are reading allows me to sell out my courses, *Mastermind*, and *high-touch 1:1 service*, all while working only the hours I choose, travelling the globe, spending time with my family and reading books. Yes, I even do it for fun. It's not only a business thing for me. Books are life. My team and I have helped hundreds of entrepreneurs' craft books, just like this one, that form the foundation of their multi-million-dollar businesses.

I want you to live the exact life you dream about. It's possible and it is available to you. The method I am sharing in this book will help you get there. I promise to share everything I know and to keep it real in every word.

If you read this book and take action, one word in front of the other, you will end up with a book that is a scalable and timeless asset for your

business – forever. I will make the process simple, fun and effective. You do not need to be a good writer. Heck, you don't even need to be able to spell a lot of fancy words. You just have to know something about something and be courageous enough to put fingers to the keyboard (or pen to paper if you prefer) and begin – and keep going.

You know stuff.

Don't overthink this thing.

Done is better than perfect.

Now, get out there. Make it happen.

"

Doing less is not being lazy. Don't give in to a culture that values personal sacrifice over personal productivity.

TIM FERRISS

ENTREPRENEUR, INVESTOR, AUTHOR, PODCASTER AND LIFESTYLE GURU

CHAPTER 2

IS THIS BOOK FOR YOU?

If you're reading this, you've probably got big dreams and ambitions for your life and business, and **you're looking for a way to step out of the hustle for clients**, leave your competitors in the dust, and shine as an industry-leading authority. Well, my friend and future bestselling author, you've come to the right place. With a book as your front-end offer, you effortlessly garner more attention and brand awareness than by fronting with one of your other products or services.

First things first though. Let's clarify who this book is for. Trust me, it's not for everyone. This book is for those of you who are ready to take your game to the next level. It's for the go-getters, the forward thinkers and the action-takers.

Let me break it down.

This book is for:

1. Entrepreneurs and business owners

If you're running your own business or thinking about it, this book is your secret weapon (actually, please don't keep it secret. Tell everyone you know – and even some you don't – awkward!). Writing a bestselling book can skyrocket your credibility, attract clients, and open doors to opportunities you never imagined.

Figure 1: The opportunities that a bestselling book can deliver for your business

2. Professionals and experts

Are you an expert in your field with years of knowledge and wisdom to share? A bestselling book can transform you into the go-to authority in your industry.

3. Creatives and artists

Maybe you're a talented artist, musician or designer. Guess what? Your creative expertise can translate into a captivating book that not only showcases your art but also establishes you as a creative visionary.

4. Coaches and consultants

If you're helping others achieve their goals, writing a bestselling book can magnify your impact. It can make you the coach or consultant with whom everyone wants to work.

5. Aspiring thought leaders

Are you eager to share your unique perspective with the world? Writing a bestselling book is your ticket to becoming a thought leader who influences minds and makes a lasting impact.

Now that we've nailed that down, let me make something else crystal clear. This book is about one thing and one thing only: helping you write a bestseller that positions you as an authority in your field. We're going to simplify your marketing, set up a steady flow of clients and opportunities coming to you on autopilot, and add a touch of star-like influence to your name.

By implementing the strategy outlined in this book, I was able to move away from being a stressed-out workaholic with a glorified job that I had created for myself, while chained to my desk at all hours of the day and night, resenting everyone and everything. Honestly, that life sucked.

By deploying a bestselling book as a key component of my business, I was able to turn my income from resembling that of an erratic coke whore into the reliable partner everyone dreams of having. Additionally, now that my income has become predictable, I no longer feel the need to deal with people who fail to light me up but rather with those I am excited to show up and work with every day.

Ultimately, I gained peace and freedom of choice. What more could a person want?

Once you finish this book and have written your own, **you will have built a marketing magnet that empowers you to choose with whom you work, to multiply your moola and to work significantly less.** We are going to show your dream clients in no uncertain terms that **you are the only person with whom they could ever want to work.**

You see in this digital age, a book is more than just words on paper. It's your golden ticket to the VIP club of industry leaders, and I'm here to guide you through every step of the process. We're going to arm you with the tools, resources and templates you need. We're going to make your book a magnet for success.

So, whether you're an entrepreneur on the rise, a seasoned professional, a creative soul, a coach or simply someone with a burning desire to share your ideas, this book is your roadmap to writing a bestseller that will change your life.

Are you ready to stop hustling for clients, outshine your competitors, and be seen as the industry-leading authority you are meant to be? If so, turn the page and let's dive in. Your bestselling book adventure has already begun.

"

The best way to predict the future is to create it.

PETER DRUCKER

MANAGEMENT CONSULTANT, EDUCATOR AND AUTHOR

CHAPTER 3

SIMPLIFY TO SCALE

To bring more ease into your life, you must be willing to stop chasing shiny things.

If you're somebody like me, you love shiny things. My counsellor reckons I have obsessive-compulsive disorder (OCD) and attention deficit hyperactivity disorder (ADHD). Honestly, I'm inclined to agree. As soon as I manage to create some sort of space in my life, I feel the need to fill it. I thrive on chaos and am always thinking of the next idea I can play with. I now understand my constant need to always be doing something as a trauma response, and I'm working on it, but that's a story for another time.

The problem with this incessant need to constantly be implementing something new and running at 100 kilometres an hour is that it isn't actually all that much fun. It's like being a hamster on a wheel that gradually gets faster and faster – you're exhausted, but you have no idea how to exit the situation that you, yourself, created. I get it.

There's no need to complicate things with endless webinars, workshops, challenges, masterclasses, or the latest marketing gimmick. The real issue is the constant pressure to create a new one every four to six weeks just to generate new leads. This relentless cycle keeps you from truly enjoying serving your clients or providing them with the quality of service or product they deserve. Instead, you're constantly focused on churning out new social media content and boosting brand awareness for your next event.

Just stop. Collaborate and listen … hmmm … really showing my age here now. But seriously …

Let it be easy.

Breathe.

You do not have to work yourself into the ground to make a lot of money. In fact, it can be just the opposite.

Too much stuff creates confusion, and confused people never buy. That chaos in which you love (but secretly loathe) operating is killing your business.

Less is more.

Simple is sexy.

Your ideal clients are already overwhelmed by life. They want clarity not an all-you-can-eat buffet of choices. They want a clear roadmap to fix their problem, and they want to be able to buy the solution easily. Just as you are reading this book to learn how to write a bestselling book that will sell out your offers and expand your business, your dream clients want the same thing. Simplicity and clarity.

All you really need is:

1. A bestselling book
2. A product or service to upsell book buyers to
3. And a sales funnel to glue the two together

As you are well aware, though, it is becoming more and more challenging to sell your offers online. Every entrepreneur and his elephant send cold direct messages (DMs), run Facebook ads and post in Facebook groups. There is nothing wrong with these strategies (except the cold DM part – please stop doing that), but they are all missing two key elements

– building trust and reducing dream client scepticism. We want to shift from forceful marketing to attraction marketing. The old way involves hustling and begging for clients. The new way has them eager and ready to buy your next-level offer without any resistance. A book is the fastest way to achieve this.

Everyone knows that at the end of a webinar, there's usually a pitch. A book, on the other hand, is the opposite. It's a pure value add - something people are eager to dive into. Your goal with your book should be to provide immense value, overdeliver, and give them everything. When you do this, it's a natural progression for readers to WANT to join your next-level offering.

A book is the ultimate authority move to influence complete strangers, indoctrinate them into your mission, and upsell them to your other offerings in just a matter of hours.

Why?

A book:

1. Showcases your expertise

Writing a book positions you as an authority in your field. It showcases your knowledge and deep understanding of the topic you are writing about. Potential clients are more likely to trust and buy from someone they perceive as an expert.

2. Provides value before purchase

By writing a book that offers valuable insights, tips or solutions to your ideal client, you give them value before they buy a higher ticket offering. This generosity creates trust and leaves the reader feeling all the good vibes toward you and your business.

3. Builds personal connection

A book allows you to share your personal journey, experiences and stories, creating a deeper and more personal connection with your readers. This is something that every human craves even if they don't realise it. By letting people peek behind the scenes of your shiny business machine and impeccable Facebook life, this human touch reduces scepticism and builds a genuine relationship with your audience.

4. Adds credibility and authority

Being a published author automatically adds credibility and authority to your name. I don't know what it is, but we humans tend to respect other humans who have taken the time to write a book and get it published. I work in the industry and still automatically trust people who have written a book – even a poor one. Go figure. The long and short of it is that people are more likely to trust and do business with someone who has authored a book, as it implies a level of commitment and expertise.

5. Differentiates

In a marketplace that is more crowded than a sardine can, having a book sets you apart from the competition. It gives potential clients a reason to choose you over others who may not have taken the time to write and share their knowledge. It makes you the golden ticket in the otherwise same, same chocolate bar selection of the Willy Wonka factory.

6. Is a content marketer

A book provides a treasure trove of content that can be repurposed for various marketing efforts. You can extract blog posts, social media updates, webinars and more from your book, further increasing your online visibility and engagement, and building on that authority. People will have no choice but to recognise that you know your stuff and that, if they have the problem you have shown you can solve, they will find a way to work with you.

7. Gives you the advantage

A book allows you to gain an unfair advantage in the marketplace. Whilst your competitors are using the outdated marketing funnels that carry high cost and friction, your book funnel has warm leads flowing in on autopilot and eager to upsell into your next level offers (refer back to Chapter 1 for a refresher on this if you need one).

8. Accelerates the pathway to sale

The quickest way to engage a new audience and convert cold traffic is through a book rich in value that highlights your expertise. Your book serves as a low-barrier introduction to you and your brand. Once readers consume the content, they will build trust and a sense of reciprocity, making them more likely to invest in your advanced offerings.

I'm certainly not saying that you will just write a book, pop it up on Amazon and be swimming in clients. Nope. Here's the thing – you still need to market it. And to avoid the hustle (ain't nobody got time for that), you need to build a simplified business ecosystem that is able to generate predictable income that requires zero of your input after it has been created. Setting up a funnel with a book as your first offering allows you to do just that.

A book on its own makes zero sense from a business standpoint, but a book implemented as part of a marketing ecosystem does. This one thing will make the difference between failure and success, losing money or making it.

A book has the power to revolutionise your business, from your conversations with potential clients to your ability to price and sell offers at a premium. However, all of this is assuming that you are getting your book into the hands of as many people as possible in a way that doesn't incur losses.

There is one problem you now need to solve. How do you get as many eyeballs as possible on your book without flushing money down the toilet?

Simply running a paid advertising campaign for your book listing on Amazon won't get you there.

Neither will sending a few emails or posting a few posts on social media.

This is because when you just send a prospect to your Amazon listing, there is no easy and obvious way for that person to move from being an interested prospect to a paying client.

Before you publish your book, you must ensure that you have your larger business strategy mapped out and ready to implement. Simply put, if you fail to leverage, you will lose.

How to stealthily capture market share

To fly under the radar and capture a significant portion of the market, you must focus on acquiring customers at a lower cost and offering them value that undercuts your competitors. When it comes to marketing and sales strategies, the Automatic Authority Method annihilates the traditional sales funnels.

Let's break down a case study to illustrate why this method is the best vehicle for skyrocketing your authority and boosting sales.

The Automatic Authority Method book funnel

- 1000 visitors go to a book sales page
- 15% buy the book at an investment of $4.97 = 150 sales and $745.50 in revenue
- 20% of the book buyers book a call to enquire about the services you promote in your book and sales funnel = 30 calls booked
- 90% of those people attend the call = 27 calls completed
- 60% of those calls result in a sale of a $3,000 package = 16 new clients and $48,000 in revenue
- Cost of ads to acquire 1000 visitors to the book sales page: $5 per click = $5,000

Net revenue: $48,745.50 (total sales + book sales) - $5,000 (ad cost) = $43,745.50

Traditional VSL/webinar funnel

- 1000 visitors go to a webinar or VSL page
- 15% attend the webinar = 150 people and $0 in revenue
- 40% of the attendees stay until the end and hear the sales pitch = 60 people pitched
- 20% of those 60 people book a call to enquire about the services you promote in your webinar or VSL = 12 calls booked
- 70% of those people attend the call = 8 calls completed

- 30% of those calls result in a sale of a $3,000 package = 3 new clients and $9,000 in revenue
- Cost of ads to acquire 1000 visitors to the VSL/webinar page: $5 per click = $5,000

Net revenue: $9,000 - $5,000 = $4,000

Now let's compare the two…

The book funnel generated $43,745.50, while the traditional VSL/webinar funnel generated $4,000. That means that the book funnel outperformed the traditional funnel by a whopping $39,745.50! That's five times the revenue of the traditional funnel! Why is this the case?

The massive difference comes down to two key factors: show-up and conversion rates as well as relationship mastery. The book funnel had a 90% show-up rate for the sales calls compared to 70% for the traditional funnel. The sales call conversion rate was 60% in the book funnel, significantly higher than the 30% in the traditional funnel. The difference in these numbers comes down to the fact that book buyers consume your message and build trust with you before hearing the pitch for your next-level offer, resulting in a deeper emotional connection to you and your brand and a higher conversion rate. Additionally, the close rate for book buyers is double that of the traditional funnel (60% vs. 30%). This is because they have already been pre-sold on you, your brand, and your next-level offer as it was promoted strategically throughout your book.

The book funnel significantly outperforms the traditional VSL/webinar funnel in terms of total revenue and conversion efficiency. By fostering trust and engagement through initial book sales, the book funnel creates a more effective pathway for high-ticket sales, demonstrating its superior value as a marketing strategy.

Book Funnel

Initial Traffic:	Book Sales:	Sales Calls:	Call Show-Up Rate:	Package Sales:
Visitors: **1000**	Conversion Rate:	Booking Rate:	Show-Up Rate:	Conversion Rate:
	15%	**20%**	**90%**	**60%**
	Sales: **150**	20% of book buyers	People Showing Up: **27**	Sales: **16**
	Price per Book: **$4.97**	Calls Booked: **30**		Price per Package: **$3,000**
	Total Revenue from Book Sales: **150 x $4.97 =**			Total Revenue from Package Sales: **16 x $3,000 =**
	$745.50			**$48,000**

Total Revenue Generated:

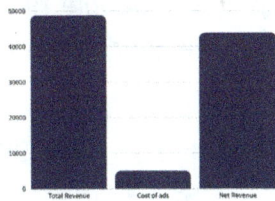

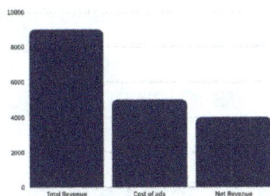

$48,745.50   **Total Revenue:** $745.50 (Book Sales) + $48,000 (Coaching Packages)

− $5,000   **Cost of ads:** $5 per click, 1,000 visitors

$43,745.50   **Net Revenue**

Traditional VSL/Webinar Funnel

Initial Traffic: Visitors: **1000**

Opt-Ins:	Engagement:	Sales Calls:	Call Show-Up Rate:	Package Sales:
Conversion Rate:	Completion Rate:	Booking Rate:	Show-Up Rate:	Conversion Rate:
15%	**40%**	**20%**	**70%**	**30%**
Opt-Ins: **150**	People Seeing Sales Message: **60**	Calls booked: **12**	People Showing Up: **8**	Sales: **3**
				Price per Package: **$3,000**
				Total Revenue from Package Sales: **3 x $3,000 =**
				$9,000

Total Revenue Generated:

$9,000   **Total Revenue:** (Coaching Packages)

− $5,000   **Cost of ads:** $5 per click, 1,000 visitors

$4,000   **Net Revenue**

Figure 2: The superiority of a book funnel over a traditional VSL/webinar funnel

A book is a low-friction purchase compared to a higher-ticket offer sold on the back end of a webinar.

Consider the steps required for a webinar sale: the prospect must attend the webinar, engage in a sales call, and then commit to a $2000+ offer. This process naturally filters out many potential buyers. In contrast, selling a book involves far less friction—people can purchase at a much lower cost and read it at their convenience.

Webinars often come with challenges like managing show-up rates and scheduling at optimal times. Even then, many people register but don't attend. Plus, hosting a webinar at an inconvenient time for you can be a hassle.

Now let's talk about the difference in the quality of leads generated by the two approaches.

Consider that out of 160 book sales, only 16 people purchase a high-ticket offering. This leaves us with 144 book buyer leads in our CRM. These leads can be strategically nurtured through email marketing with case studies, video testimonials, additional value content, client success stories, and more until they are ready to buy. Because these individuals have read your book and built an affinity for you, the email open rates will be significantly higher than traditional email marketing metrics.

In contrast, with a webinar funnel, those who don't book a call are likely to forget about you, especially if they didn't watch the webinar until the end. They are more likely to ignore your emails and reject your future sales messages because they haven't developed the know, like, and trust factor with you and your brand. This results in lower email open rates and engagement.

Therefore, the quality of your email database and the effectiveness of marketing your future offers are vastly different between the two funnels. If you want predictable revenue and aim to have magnetic marketing that effortlessly sells people into your next-level offers, the Automatic Authority book funnel is far superior.

In essence, this argument boils down to the quality of the leads on both lists. With the book funnel, you have a lead list of customers to email market to, whereas the webinar funnels leave you with a list of freebie seekers who are not indoctrinated into your brand and business offerings.

Next up, let's get into sales call dynamics, a difference so potent it requires its own section!

Sales call dynamics

VSL/webinar funnels vs. Automatic Authority funnels

When it comes to sales calls, the approach and atmosphere can vary significantly depending on the type of funnel being used. I'm going to show you why, once again, the Automatic Authority funnel is the only way you want to be selling from now on...

VSL/webinar sales calls: the push and force approach

VSL/webinar funnels often require a more aggressive sales strategy. The sales calls resulting from these funnels typically involve a lot of push and force. Here's what you can expect:

1. Duration

These calls generally last between 60 to 90 minutes. The extended time is needed to build rapport, understand the prospect, provide detailed explanations of the solution being sold, handle objections, and persuade the prospect to make a purchase.

2. Sales tactics

The sales tactics used in VSL/webinar funnels are often hard and direct. Sales representatives may use a combination of urgency, scarcity, and various closing techniques to push the prospect towards a decision.

3. Intensity

The calls are high-pressure and can be emotionally intense for both the salesperson and the prospect. The goal is to convert the prospect by the end of the call, leading to a heavy focus on closing the deal.

4. Prospect engagement

Prospects may feel they need more convincing and may have more reservations, leading to a more prolonged and intense discussion.

Automatic Authority sales calls:
the calm, confident and effortless approach

In contrast, sales calls resulting from the Automatic Authority funnels are typically shorter and more relaxed. By the time book buyers get on a sales call to potentially invest in your next level offering, they already know, like, and trust you, which changes the dynamic of the sales call:

1. Duration

These calls usually last between 15 to 30 minutes. The brevity is due to the prospect already being pre-sold on the value and authority of the offering.

2. Sales tactics

The tactics used in these calls are softer and really more of a consult than a sale. The sales representative's role is to answer a few clarifying questions and provide additional information as needed rather than to push for a sale.

3. Intensity

The calls are low-pressure and focused on ensuring the prospect feels comfortable and confident in their decision to buy. The environment is more conversational and less confrontational.

4. Prospect engagement

Prospects coming through an Automatic Authority funnel are usually more informed and ready to buy. They see the call as an opportunity to clarify details rather than being convinced to make a purchase.

Key differences and implications

The stark differences between the two types of sales calls highlight the importance of the funnel strategy you choose. Webinar funnels can be exhausting and require skilled salespeople to manage the high-pressure environment.

On the other hand, Automatic Authority funnels are ideal for creating a seamless and efficient sales process. They position the salesperson as an expert, making the sales call more about providing value and answering questions, thus leading to quicker and often more pleasant interactions.

VSL/WEBINAR FUNNEL SALES CALLS		AUTOMATIC AUTHORITY BOOK FUNNEL SALES CALLS
60 to 90 minutes	Duration	15 to 30 minutes
Hard and direct	Tactics	Easy and conversational
High-pressure and emotionally charged	Intensity	Low-pressure and conversational
Need convincing and have more reservations	Prospect engagement	Informed and ready to buy
Push and force	Approach	Calm, confident and effortless

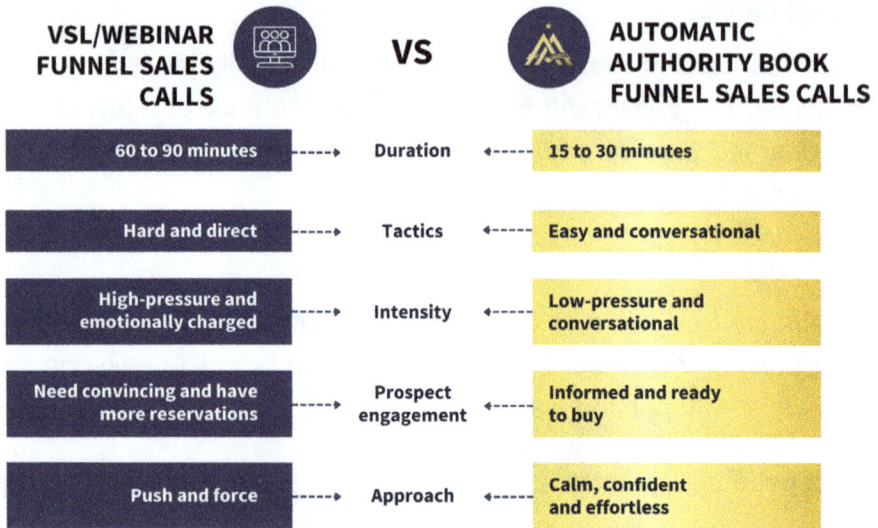

Figure 3: Sales call dynamics

If you have clients on the other side of the world, you no longer need to take late-night sales calls with cold prospects who might say no at 1 am. Instead, let your book do the selling for you, attracting high-ticket clients on autopilot.

During webinars, attendees can easily get distracted by other tabs and interruptions. However, a book offers a timeless, distraction-free experience that readers can enjoy in their own time and special quiet place.

A book is a lasting asset that they can consume and revisit as often as they like. If it's a hard copy, it remains constantly in their view and on their mind, which means YOU are on their mind.

Here's the strategy: Run paid ads and/or send all your organic marketing channels to your sales funnel with your book as the front-end offer. The book helps potential customers get to know, like, and trust you. From there, you can upsell them to higher-value offers such as coaching, memberships, retreats, or subscriptions/software.

Additionally, you have the opportunity to realise something your competitors don't! In the world of marketing, experts like Sabri Suby highlight a critical insight: in any given market, only 3% of potential customers are ready to buy at any given moment. This statistic might seem daunting, but it reveals a significant opportunity for savvy businesses willing to look beyond the obvious.

Understanding the market segments

To understand why this 3% figure is so important, let's break down the market:

1. **3% Ready to Buy:** This tiny fraction is actively seeking a solution and is ready to purchase now.
2. **17% Information Gathering:** These individuals recognise they have a problem and are researching solutions, comparing options, and preparing to make a decision.
3. **20% Problem Awareness:** This segment knows they have a problem but haven't started looking for solutions yet.
4. **60% Unaware of the Problem:** The largest group doesn't even realise they have a problem that needs solving.

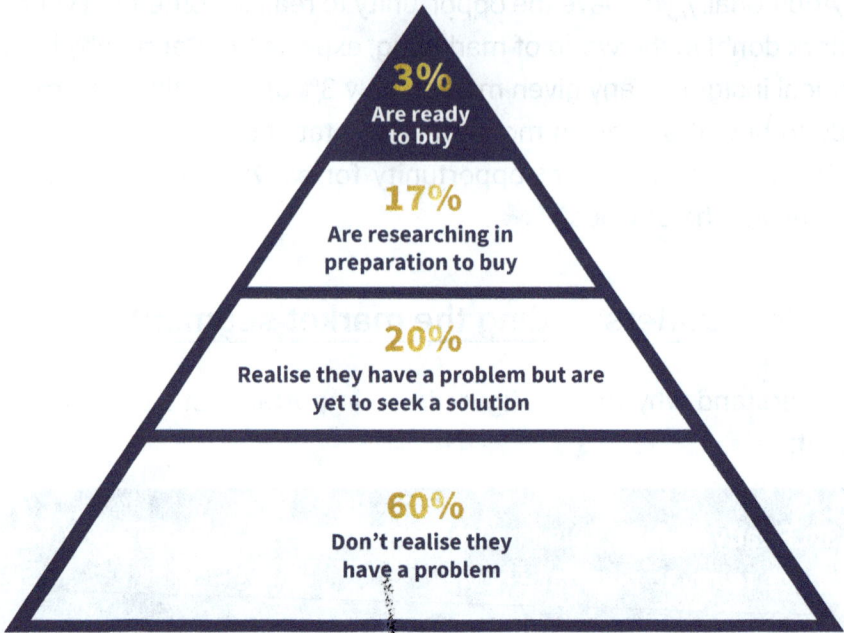

Figure 4: The reality of the market

The common mistake: focusing on the 3%

Most businesses direct their advertising efforts toward the 3% who are ready to buy. Their messages scream, "Buy my stuff now!" While this might seem logical, it's also highly competitive and costly. Everyone is vying for the attention of this small segment, driving up advertising costs and reducing the effectiveness of each campaign.

The untapped opportunity: the other 97%

Now, imagine shifting your focus to the remaining 97% of the market. Here's how targeting these groups can transform your marketing strategy:

1. The 17% information gatherers

Craft content in both your book and social channels that educates and informs. Provide detailed guides, comparisons, and testimonials to help these potential customers make informed decisions. By positioning yourself as a trusted source of information, you become the logical choice when they are ready to buy.

2. The 20% problem aware

Develop awareness campaigns on your social media that highlight the issues they face and introduce the solution (delivered through your book) as the answer. Use storytelling to emotionally connect and illustrate how your product or service can improve their situation.

3. The 60% unaware

This is the trickiest segment, but also the most rewarding. Create engaging content that highlights common pain points and subtly introduces the problems they might not realise they have. Use social proof, case studies, and relatable scenarios to gently nudge them towards recognising their need for your solution.

The benefits of a broader focus

By targeting the 97%, you'll:

1. Lower acquisition costs

With less competition for attention, your advertising dollars stretch further.

2. Build brand loyalty

Establishing trust and providing value before the sales pitch creates a strong foundation for long-term customer relationships.

3. Increase market share

As your competitors scramble over the 3%, you quietly gain a larger share of the market by converting those who were previously overlooked.

When you target the broader market, you effectively "steal" market share from your competitors. They remain focused on the small, highly competitive segment, while you cultivate relationships and build a robust customer base from the ground up.

Embracing the Blue Ocean Strategy

To further understand the potential of targeting the broader market, let's dive into the Blue Ocean Strategy (pun totally intended), a concept introduced by W. Chan Kin and Renée Mauborgne. This strategy divides the market into two distinct types of oceans:

1. Red ocean

These are the existing market spaces where competition is fierce, and businesses fight over the same, limited pool of customers. It's bloodthirsty with competition, driving down profits and creating a struggle for business survival.

2. Blue ocean

These are the untapped market spaces where competition is irrelevant because the rules of the game are yet to be set. It's about creating and capturing new demand, making the competition obsolete.

Most businesses are competing in the red ocean, vying for the attention of the same 3% of customers who are ready to buy. This results in a zero-sum game where one business's gain is another's loss. By adopting a blue ocean strategy, you shift your focus away from the bloody waters of competition and towards creating new market space.

Creating low-cost, low-friction solutions

One way to achieve this is by creating offerings that are low-cost and low friction. For example, developing a book that:

1. Educates and engages

Target those who are aware of their problem but need more information (the 17% information gatherers).

2. Increases awareness

Address the 20% who know they have a problem but haven't started seeking solutions.

3. Reveals hidden problems

Subtly inform the 60% who are unaware of their problems through relatable content and stories.

Dominating the orange and blue oceans

By targeting these segments, you not only capture the increasingly competitive "orange ocean" but also begin to explore and dominate the "blue ocean." Here's how this strategy works:

1. Orange ocean (increasingly competitive)

As you target the 97% you gradually turn this market into an orange ocean. It becomes more competitive but still holds vast opportunities compared to the red ocean. Your early presence and established trust give you a competitive edge.

2. Blue ocean (uncontested waters)

By addressing the needs and problems that customers aren't even aware of, you create a new demand. This uncontested market space allows you to set the rules, capture the market share, and enjoy higher profitability without the cutthroat competition.

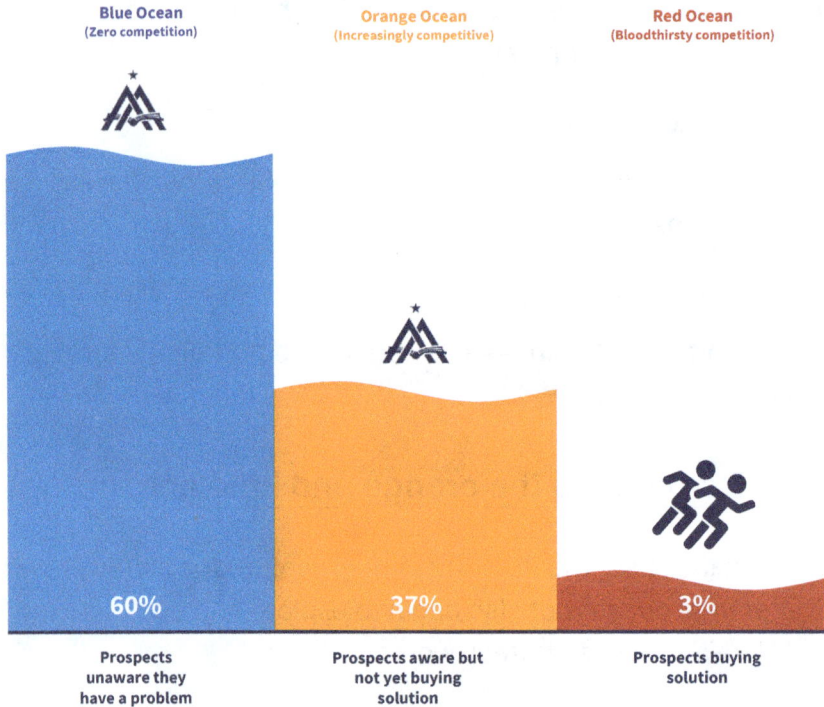

Blue Ocean
(Zero competition)

Orange Ocean
(Increasingly competitive)

Red Ocean
(Bloodthirsty competition)

60%

37%

3%

Prospects
unaware they
have a problem

Prospects aware but
not yet buying
solution

Prospects buying
solution

Figure 5: Your playground of possibility

While your competitors focus on driving traffic to webinars, events, or free eBooks (which often go unread), you leverage a compelling, bestselling book to engage and convert your audience. This approach not only builds credibility but also strategically guides customers towards more lucrative offerings.

The key idea is to structure your business so that the math works overwhelmingly in your favour, ensuring success even if your marketing or operations aren't perfect.

The strategy involves selling a low-cost book that contains immense value and then using an automated sales funnel to guide buyers into your next level back-end offers, be it a course, membership, software, or high-ticket 1-on-1 or group coaching experience. Here's how you can implement this:

1. Begin with the end in mind

Understand what you aim to sell to your readers: Is it a course, a membership, software, high-ticket group or individual coaching, or a done-for-you service? Once you have a clear vision of your next-level offers, you can seamlessly incorporate them into your book. By the time readers finish the last page, they'll be excited to enrol in your next-level offer.

2. Break even on the front end

Determine which three to five order bumps you will offer when someone purchases your book. This will help you break even or even profit from the initial sale, ensuring that any subsequent upsells are pure profit. Can you create an audiobook version? How about a fast start or rapid launch masterclass or mini-course that compliments your book's topic? Could you offer cheat sheets or templates to help your readers achieve their goals more effectively?

3. Create a unique book

Develop a book with a unique angle that stands out in the market. Ensure it offers real, usable value and gives away as much as possible to ensure the reader can implement what you are teaching.

4. Build the funnel

Construct a sales funnel around your book, including a compelling sales page that converts at around 10-15%.

5. Run ads and implement organic marketing

Drive traffic to your book sales page through ads or organic marketing strategies. If you can allocate a budget of $50/day for paid ads, amazing! If not, consider guest podcasting, creating social media content, and engaging in strategic collaborations and joint ventures to achieve great results.

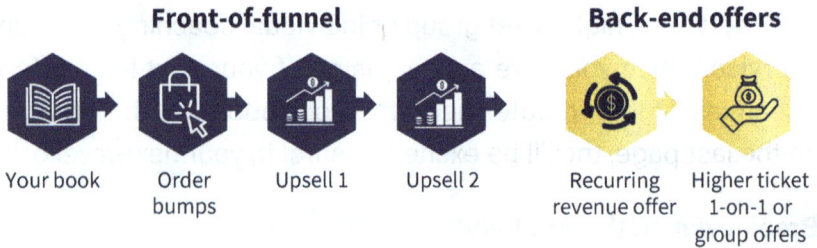

Figure 6: Your authority-building ecosystem

Your book should deliver genuine value, positioning it as a core product that not only breaks even on customer acquisition costs but also generates significant revenue from day one. By strategically placing optional upgrades, such as order bumps and recurring revenue offers, alongside two or three substantial upsells, you can optimise profitability.

This approach enables you to acquire 50-300+ new front-end paying customers daily while building a loyal community. Providing massive value and building trust will strengthen relationships with each customer.

Your next step will be to segment your customers into different groups and create an awareness process to move them seamlessly through your offerings. Think targeted email campaigns, retargeted ads, direct warm outreach and so on.

You may choose to offer implementation support for what you are teaching and consider done-for-you options as your larger upsells.

IDEAL READER AVATAR

Sees ad

Clicks to book sales page

Purchases book + potential order bumps

Proceeds through upsell path

Thank you page

Delivery of products

Product experience

Loyal customer eager to upsell into your next level offerings

LOYAL BRAND AMBASSADOR

Figure 7: Your loyal fan generation machine

Repeat and optimise this process continually. By competing on this level, your business can achieve unparalleled success. Your book should solve a problem for your audience whilst also bringing another pressing problem into their awareness, so it triggers the urgency in them to enrol in your next level offers.

Once your book provides the complete solution to your client's initial problem, a new challenge often emerges, such as implementing the work to achieve the desired transformation. Your next step is to identify the immediate problem that arises from the initial solution and turn your response into your first upsell. This allows the client to purchase the next solution and continue progressing, solving subsequent problems with your successive upsells.

Within your funnel, some clients will seek to implement solutions quickly and effectively. This is where your higher ticket offers become essential. You can provide a range of options, such as self-paced courses, masterminds, or done-for-you services, to help them achieve their goals efficiently.

By implementing this ecosystem, you unlock endless possibilities and position yourself as a dominant force in your industry.

Companies like Google, Facebook, and YouTube achieve their massive success and market dominance by giving away their best content for free and generating revenue through other avenues within their systems.

This model's success lies in its approach of starting small with a low-cost, low-risk solution—a book. Instead of asking for a significant investment from a cold audience, you begin by offering an affordable and easy-to-commit-to solution to their problem. This strategy essentially allows you to "buy" new relationships at scale. Purchasing a book is a minimal investment for most people, making it an easy decision. You're not asking your potential prospects to commit heavily upfront; instead, you're building a relationship with them. By offering your book first, you demonstrate why you are the right person to help them, fostering trust and paving the way for future, higher value offers.

Real-life examples

Let's look at some examples of successful entrepreneurs who are using books as their front-end offers to make huge amounts of money on the back end...

Sabri Suby, founder of King Kong

Sabri Suby, founder of King Kong, a digital marketing agency, uses his book, *Sell Like Crazy*, as a strategic tool to generate leads and grow his authority in the industry. Here's how he accomplishes this:

1. Providing value

Suby's book offers valuable insights and actionable strategies for businesses looking to improve their marketing efforts. By sharing his expertise and proven methods, he establishes himself as an authority in digital marketing.

2. Lead generation

The book acts as a lead magnet. Readers interested in his insights are likely to visit his website or sign up for a strategy session with his team, to learn more about how his agency and courses can help them grow their business. This helps build a list of potential clients who have already shown interest in his services.

3. Building trust

By delivering high-quality content and practical advice in his book, Suby builds trust with his audience. This trust makes potential clients more likely to engage with his agency for their marketing needs.

4. Upselling services

Throughout his book, Suby subtly promotes his agency's services by demonstrating the success his strategies have brought to other clients. This positions King Kong as the go-to solution for readers who want to implement the techniques discussed.

5. Expanding reach

Publishing a book allows Suby to reach a broader audience beyond digital channels. It helps him tap into traditional media and book promotion opportunities, further expanding his influence and attracting new leads.

6. Enhanced credibility

The success and popularity of Sabri's book have significantly enhanced his credibility as a marketing expert. This credibility makes him a desirable guest on shows like *Shark Tank*, where authoritative and successful entrepreneurs are sought after.

7. Media exposure

The impact of his book has attracted media attention, leading to interviews, guest articles, and features in prominent publications. This media exposure increases visibility and positions him as an industry leader, making him a natural choice for television appearances.

8. Networking opportunities

As an established author and authority, Suby has access to high-level networking opportunities. Engaging with influential business figures and media personalities can lead to invitations to participate in shows like *Shark Tank*.

9. Content marketing

The book provides a wealth of content that can be repurposed for blogs, social media, webinars, and other marketing channels, ensuring consistent visibility and engagement with his target audience.

Overall, by leveraging his book as a comprehensive marketing tool, Sabri Suby effectively generates leads, builds his authority, and drives growth for his business.

Alex Hormozi, entrepreneur, investor, and author

Alex Hormozi, a successful entrepreneur and business advisor, has effectively used books to generate leads for his business and grow his authority in the entrepreneurial space. Here's how he has accomplished this:

1. High-value content

Hormozi's books, such as *100M Offers and 100M Leads,* provide substantial value to readers by sharing actionable insights and strategies drawn from his own experiences. This high-quality content not only helps readers but also positions Hormozi as an authority in the business and marketing fields.

2. Free book offers

Hormozi often offers his books for free, requiring only that readers cover shipping costs. This strategy lowers the barrier to entry for potential readers, encouraging more people to get his book. In return, Hormozi collects contact information from those who order, which he can then use for follow-up marketing.

3. Upsell funnels

When readers sign up for a free book, they often enter a sales funnel where they are presented with additional offers. These offers can include advanced training programs, courses, or consulting services. This not only increases revenue but also moves leads further down the sales funnel. I recently bought his collector's edition set of *$100M Leads,* which included three hardcover books and a branded hat. My French Bulldog Pierre ate the hat that very weekend.

4. Leveraging social proof

Hormozi's book launches are accompanied by significant social proof, including testimonials, reviews, and case studies from successful clients. This builds credibility and encourages others to trust his expertise.

5. Omnipresent marketing

He promotes his books across various platforms, including social media, podcasts, YouTube, and email marketing. By being omnipresent, Hormozi ensures that his message reaches a broad audience, increasing the chances of his book being noticed and shared.

6. Strategic partnerships

Hormozi collaborates with influencers and other entrepreneurs to promote his books. He leverages affiliate marketers to help him get more traffic to his book sales pages and therefore, more sales which are already backed by social proof from the affiliates. These partnerships expand his reach and tap into new audiences who trust the recommendations of these influencers.

7. Content repurposing

Content from his books is often repurposed into blog posts, videos, and social media snippets. This continuous stream of content keeps his audience engaged and reinforces his authority on the subject matter.

8. Building a personal brand

Through his books, Hormozi not only promotes his business but also builds his personal brand. By consistently providing valuable content and sharing his journey, he creates a strong personal connection with his audience.

9. Successful book launches

Hormozi's book launches are meticulously planned and executed, often involving pre-launch marketing, exclusive offers, and leveraging his existing audience to create buzz. These launches often result in massive sales and a significant influx of leads, making them some of the most successful book launches in the entrepreneurial space.

By using these strategies, Alex Hormozi has turned his books into powerful tools for lead generation and authority building, contributing significantly to the growth and success of his business ventures.

Gabby Bernstein, author, motivational speaker, and podcast host

Gabby Bernstein effectively uses her books as front-end offers to sell her other services and build her brand through several strategic methods:

1. High-value content

Bernstein's books provide valuable insights, personal stories, and practical advice that resonate with her target audience. This builds trust and positions her as an authority in the self-help and spiritual growth space.

2. Call to action

Throughout her books, she includes calls to action that direct readers to her website, social media platforms, and other online resources. These CTAs often encourage readers to sign up for her newsletter, join her online communities, or attend her events.

3. Consistent messaging

The themes and messages in her books align with her overall brand, reinforcing her identity as a spiritual leader and motivational speaker. This consistency helps create a strong, recognizable brand.

4. Personal connection

Bernstein shares personal anecdotes and experiences in her books, which helps readers feel a deeper connection to her. This personal touch enhances her brand's relatability and authenticity.

5. Workshops and retreats

After establishing trust through her books, Bernstein promotes her workshops, retreats, and seminars. Readers who find value in her books are more likely to invest in these higher-ticket services for more in-depth learning and personal development.

6. Online courses and memberships

She offers online courses and memberships that provide ongoing support and deeper dives into the topics covered in her books. These are marketed as logical next steps for readers seeking more comprehensive guidance.

7. Interactive content

Bernstein often includes links to downloadable resources, guided meditations, and exercises that complement her books. This interactive content keeps readers engaged and drives them to her online platforms where she can capture their details and further develop a relationship with potential clients.

8. Social media and live events

She leverages her social media presence to connect with readers, offering live events, Q&A sessions, and community support. This fosters a sense of belonging and encourages readers to stay engaged with her brand.

9. Collaborations and partnerships

Bernstein collaborates with other influencers and brands in the self-help space. This cross-promotion helps her reach new audiences and build credibility through association.

10. Media appearances

She frequently appears on podcasts, television shows, and in interviews where she discusses her books and other services. These appearances help expand her reach and attract new potential clients.

11. Email marketing

Bernstein uses email marketing to nurture leads generated from her book promotions. She provides additional value through exclusive content, updates, and offers tailored to her audience's interests.

12. Retargeting campaigns

She employs retargeting ads to reach individuals who have shown interest in her books but haven't yet engaged with her other services. These campaigns often highlight testimonials and success stories to encourage conversion.

13. Feedback and testimonials

Bernstein collects and showcases testimonials from readers who have benefited from her books and services. This social proof reinforces the effectiveness of her offerings and encourages repeat purchases.

14. Ongoing engagement

She maintains ongoing communication with her audience through news-letter, social media updates, and follow-up content, ensuring her brand remains top-of-mind and fostering long-term loyalty.

Through these strategies, Gabby Bernstein effectively uses her books as entry points to a broader ecosystem of services, creating a holistic brand experience that drives engagement, loyalty, and revenue growth.

As you can see, these three successful entrepreneurs are using books as their front-end offers to drive traffic through their larger eco-system of offers. They make a lot of money and position themselves as industry authorities whilst they do it. Writing a book and leveraging it is not only available to entrepreneurial giants like these. You can implement this exact ecosystem too and that's exactly what I'm going to help you with right now.

> *Marketing used to be about making a myth and telling it. Now it's about telling a truth and sharing it.*

MARC MATHIEU

CO-FOUNDER OF SALESFORCE

CHAPTER 4

WRITING YOUR BOOK WITHIN 28 DAYS

I can hear the sceptical voices in your head asking, 'Is writing a book in 28 days even possible?' Yes, my friend, it is (bearing in mind that I wrote this book in a week). It's going to take some dedication, a dash of discipline and a sprinkle of creativity, but I promise you it can be done.

If you need a little ass-kickery to ensure you do it, don't forget to join our community by scanning the QR code at the end of Chapter 20. Either that, or work with us inside one of our other containers. Hell, we can even write your book for you. But for now, let's begin the business of how you can get your own book written in 28 days or less.

The purpose of your book

First, I'm going to be blunt. Your readers are not buying your book for entertainment. This isn't some casual read they are after. Your book is about convincing them that you're the expert who can help them. So, when you're putting pen to paper – or fingers to keyboard – aim for clarity, keep it concise and be straight to the point.

And here's a little secret: your ideas matter more than your writing style. Most readers are cruising along at a junior school reading level, which is pretty much like having a chat, so don't panic.

Setting the stage

Let's start with a reality check. Your calendar is probably jam-packed with work commitments, family obligations and the occasional Netflix binge. I'm not asking you to give all of this up, but guess what? If you want this book to happen, you've got to carve out some sacred writing time. Maybe it's just an hour before the world wakes up, or perhaps it's a late-night rendezvous with your laptop.

Whatever it is, mark it in your calendar like it's a hot date. Because, let's face it, this book is your new love affair.

Check out Chapter 5 for more tips on how to find time to write.

Embrace the mess

Writing is messy. Your first draft is not going to be a literary masterpiece. It's going to be a bit like a Jackson Pollock painting – a splatter of ideas, concepts and sentences that may or may not make sense. Embrace it! This is not the time for perfectionism. This is the time for getting your thoughts out of your head and onto the page.

Set realistic goals

Break down your writing process into manageable chunks. If you're aiming for a 60,000-word book in 28 days, that's roughly 2,142 words a day. Easy, right? On those days when the words flow effortlessly, you'll surpass that goal. On the days when every word feels like a tooth extraction, you'll at least hit your minimum. Celebrate the small victories.

Tame the inner editor

The inner editor is that annoying voice in your head that tells you everything you're writing is garbage. Ignore it.

In the 'first bad draft' your goal is quantity not quality. There will be plenty of time for editing later. Right now, focus on getting the ideas out. Remember, you can't edit a blank page. It's not your job to edit anyway. That's what you will get a structural editor for when it's time for your manuscript to go through the publishing process.

Some people out there will encourage you to edit your own work. I'm not one of those people. Get out of your own way and hand it to a professional. People get degrees in editing and if you want the quality of book that sells and enhances your reputation (rather than damaging it), get an editor. We both know you will only procrastinate around getting it perfect anyway.

Outsource your motivation

Find an accountability partner (see Bonus Chapter 2). Share your goals with them and let them hold you accountable. Knowing that someone else is expecting you to deliver can be a powerful motivator.

The Pomodoro Technique is your friend

The Pomodoro Technique is a time management method where you work in short, focused bursts, typically 25 minutes followed by a short break. Set a timer, write like the wind for 25 minutes, take a break, repeat. It's amazing how much you can accomplish when you're racing against the clock.

Embrace the rewrite

Once your first draft is done, take a breather. Then, come back to it with fresh eyes. The real magic happens in the rewriting. Don't be afraid to cut, add and reshape. (I swapped chapters around in this book about 12 times as I was writing it.) Your first draft is the raw material and the subsequent drafts are where you sculpt your masterpiece.

Rally your cheerleaders

As you approach the finish line, share your progress with friends and family. Their excitement and encouragement can be the fuel you need to power through those final chapters. Plus, it's a built-in fan club for your upcoming book launch!

Getting your non-fiction book written in 28 days is no small feat, but it's absolutely doable. Remember, this isn't about writing the perfect book, it's about writing a book. So, set a start date, unleash your creativity, banish procrastination and make those 28 days count.

"

The only limit to the height of your achievements is the reach of your dreams and your willingness to work for them.

MICHELLE OBAMA

LAWYER AND AUTHOR

CHAPTER 5

FINDING THE TIME TO WRITE
Maximising Productivity and Creativity

To write a book within 28 days requires more than just discipline. It demands a strategic approach to harnessing your productivity and creativity. In the perpetual hustle and bustle of modern life, finding time to sit down and write can often seem like an elusive venture.

However, if you wish to get your book written so you can sort out your marketing, get back to living your life and have pre-qualified leads clamouring to give you their money all year round, then write you must. Armed with a dash of creativity, some strategic organisation and a commitment to a writing routine, you will be able to give life to your book.

This chapter delves into establishing rituals and habits that not only foster a conducive writing environment but also ignite your creative spark, ensuring that each writing session is as productive as possible.

The power of rituals in writing

Rituals are more than mere routines. They are intentional practices that prepare your mind and body for the task at hand. In this context, rituals signal to your brain that it's time to focus on shifting gears from the chaos of daily life to the clarity and concentration required for writing.

Whether it's a cup of coffee in your favourite mug (we have some awesome mugs in our online store!), a brief meditation or a specific play-list, these rituals create a psychological trigger that enhances focus and productivity.

Crafting your ideal writing environment

Your environment plays a critical role in you writing productively. It should be a sanctuary where your creativity can flourish without distractions. Consider factors such as lighting, noise levels and comfort. Some writers thrive in the quiet seclusion of a home office, while others find inspiration in the buzz of a local cafe. Experiment to find the environment that best suits your writing style and maximises your productivity.

Establishing a consistent writing schedule

Consistency is key to completing your book on schedule. Set aside dedicated writing times each day or week, treating these as non-negotiable appointments with yourself. Early mornings may work best for some, capitalising on the brain's fresh, creative energy, while others may find their writing stride in the quiet of the night.

Whichever you choose, consistency in your writing schedule is crucial for maintaining momentum and making steady progress.

Early morning serenity

Waking early might seem a daunting prospect, especially for those who identify as night owls. Personally, I'm an early bird but I haven't had a full night's sleep in almost eight years. My daughter is eight and still doesn't sleep through the night, so I understand how maybe you would prefer to get shot in the kneecaps than get up early but hear me out.

The quietude of the early morning hours provides an undisturbed sanctuary for your creative thoughts. Picture the children still asleep, the house quiet for once, the world still draped in dawn's tranquillity as you sip your coffee or tea, with the only sounds being the tap of your keyboard or the scratch of your pen. My nervous system just breathed a sigh of relief!

This early writing ritual not only allows you to jump start your day with a sense of accomplishment but it also nurtures a peaceful environment for your creative musings.

Lunch break escapade

If mornings are too chaotic or you simply can't drag yourself out of bed, then the lunch break offers a perfect interlude for a rendezvous with your writing. Stepping away from your workspace, immersing yourself in a change of scenery and using that time to pen your thoughts can be both refreshing and productive.

It's a dual-purpose strategy, allowing you to nurture your physical wellbeing with fresh air and exercise while also feeding your purpose of writing.

Twilight writing sessions

For those who find solace in the stillness of the evening (not me, I'm in bed by 7:30 some nights), setting aside time after dinner or before bedtime can be an ideal slot for writing. As the day winds down, creating a writing sanctuary free from electronic distractions allows you to focus entirely on your book. This time also serves as a reflective period which you can channel into your creative work.

Setting realistic goals and deadlines

Goal setting is an effective way to stay on track, but it's important to be realistic. Setting daily or weekly wordcount targets can be motivating but these goals should be achievable, taking into account your writing speed, available time and other commitments. Break down your book into smaller, manageable sections and set deadlines for each, allowing for flexibility to adjust as needed.

Strategic scheduling and shared responsibilities

The key to unlocking additional writing time lies in strategic planning (celebrate with me, fellow nerds!). You'll be surprised by the amount of time you can recover in your schedule by planning. Let me give you some personal examples:

- On a Monday I drop my daughter at dancing for 40 minutes. By the time I drop her off and get home I can fit in 30 minutes of writing time.
- On a Tuesday I have arranged for my daughter to go to her friend's house for an hour after school, giving me 60 minutes of writing time.
- On a Wednesday I take my daughter to swimming for 30 minutes. That's a half hour of writing time while I sit and wait for her to finish.
- On a Thursday night I take my daughter to dancing again a few towns over and have to wait in the car for her. There is another 40 minutes of writing time.

I have also arranged with another school mum who runs her own business to share the school drop-offs and pick-ups each week. We do half each. It takes me 30 minutes (in good traffic) each way to the school, which is a total of two hours a day. So, on days when my friend does the school run, I gain an extra two hours. Golden writing time.

You can see how seemingly routine activities, like dropping off or picking up children, can be transformed into invaluable writing windows. Collaborating with others like this is a brilliant way to optimise your schedule. By sharing responsibilities, you not only gain back precious hours, but you also create a supportive community conducive to your work.

Expanding the definition of writing time

Now, writing doesn't solely mean putting pen to paper, so let's take a broader perspective. Whether it's jotting down ideas on your smartphone during a commute or brainstorming additional resources while waiting for a child's after-school activity to finish, these moments can all contribute to your writing journey.

With a dash of ingenuity and a commitment to a structured routine, you can unearth precious pockets of time for writing amid the whirlwind of daily life. So, drop the excuse that you are too busy, embrace the challenge, get creative and start writing – today.

Coming up, I share my Finding the Pockets of Time in Your Week guide to help you further refine your time management skills and enhance your writing journey. Let's do it.

"

You will never find time for anything. If you want time you must make it.

CHARLES BUXTON

ENGLISH BREWER, WRITER, PHILANTHROPIST AND MP

Finding the pockets of time in your week

Objective: To use this guide to help you identify where you can fit in time to write.

Your week

Fill in the calendar below with your commitments for this week (both personal and professional):

SUN	MON	TUE	WED	THU	FRI	SAT

Taking a closer look

1. Are there any free time slots that you could schedule in some writing time?
2. Looking at your calendar, can you identify any commitments that require you to spend time waiting, such as at your child's sports game?
3. Check your commitments and identify those you can do without. Cancel them or delegate them to someone else. List these and include the action you will take and your deadline for taking care of them.

Your upgraded calendar

Now that you have identified the extra pockets of time in your day, add them to your weekly calendar below along with your other commitments. Dedicate these newfound pockets of time as sacred writing time. Get your book written.

SUN	MON	TUE	WED	THU	FRI	SAT

You can do this exercise on a piece of paper, or if you'd like to download a digital version of this worksheet, scan the QR code below:

CHAPTER 6

AUTHOR MYTHS

There are many myths and misconceptions about what it takes to be an author. Some people think that you have to be a genius to write a book or that you need to know someone in the publishing industry. In this chapter, we will dispel some of the most common myths about authorship and further teach you how to become a successful author.

You need to be a genius to write a book

This simply isn't true. Anyone can write a book as long as they have something to say. The key to writing a successful book is not your IQ but your ability to communicate your ideas clearly and effectively.

The notion that you need to be super smart to write a book is not only unfounded but one that discourages many aspiring writers. It comes down to your passion and dedication to communicate your ideas in a compelling and coherent way.

Many epic writers are known for their ability to connect with readers on an emotional level, sharing insights, stories and perspectives that resonate rather than relying solely on intellectual prowess.

The essence of writing lies in the art of effective communication – something we entrepreneurs have to become very good at to connect with our dream clients. You may possess a wealth of knowledge but the true challenge you face is conveying that knowledge in a way that captivates an audience or engages a client.

The beauty of writing is that it allows for diverse voices and perspectives, making room for those who may not consider themselves geniuses but who still have valuable experiences, insights or stories to share.

Embrace your unique voice, cultivate your communication skills and get those fingers writing or typing that book to bring your ideas to life.

You need to know someone in the publishing industry

This isn't true either. In the rapidly changing world of the publishing industry, the age-old notion that you need to have connections or know someone 'on the inside' to get your book published is obsolete. The rise of self-publishing (I have a course on this, if you're interested!) has democratised the process, allowing aspiring authors to bring their stories to life independently.

Self-publishing has opened a world of opportunities that allow writers to retain creative control, set their own timelines and keep a large share of the profits. However, it's important to understand that while self-publishing eliminates the need for traditional gatekeepers, it doesn't remove the challenges of producing a polished and marketable book.

You only need to look on Amazon to see some horrendous books thrown up by self-published authors. A poor-quality book will damage your business, not enhance it.

Choosing to self-publish demands a huge commitment of time, effort and resources (including money). Authors must wear multiple hats, taking on roles beyond just writing, such as hiring the right editors, typesetters, designers, etc, as well as taking on marketing and distribution.

For those who are passionate about their work but prefer not to handle every aspect of the publishing process alone, hybrid publishers offer a middle ground. Companies like mine provide a bridge between traditional and self-publishing. Hybrids offer a range of services delivered by experts while allowing authors to maintain creative control.

If you are willing to put in the effort, then self-publishing may be right for you. Otherwise, you have the option of working with a hybrid publisher, like us here at Automatic Authority Publishing & Press House, or try your luck with a traditional publisher.

Writing a book is expensive

Writing a book doesn't have to be expensive but it is naive to think it won't cost anything. The key is to consider your needs, do your research and find the option that best suits them. Some people want their book written for them. Some people need to work with a book coach. Some need to use paid versions of writing tools.

Writing a book can be labour-intensive but it primarily demands your time (we showed you how to leverage your time to fast-track the process in Chapter 5) and creative energy. It really comes down to a dance of time vs money vs expertise.

You need to be a great writer to be an author

You don't need to be a published author or have a degree in writing to write a book. Hell, you don't even have to be particularly good at spelling or have English as your first language. In fact, many successful authors started as novice writers. The most important thing is having a good idea and being willing to work hard.

You need to put life on hold to write a book

While it is important to set aside time for writing, you don't need to quit your job, spend every day in the library or take an entire month out to sit in a cabin in the woods with a typewriter to write a book. In fact, many authors find they are more productive when they establish specific writing goals and deadlines.

Contrary to the romanticised image of a writer sequestered in isolation, surrounded by nothing but the rustling of leaves in a remote cabin (a girl can dream) or the hushed ambience of a library, the reality is that effective writing can co-exist with a vibrant, engaged life. In fact, as I write these words, I am surrounded by the background noise of cartoons on the TV, my Frenchie's snores, and my daughter asking if she can have yet another yoghurt.

The key to getting your book down is not to abandon life as you currently know it, but to strike a balance that allows creativity to flourish despite the demands of daily life. Maintaining a business, family commitments, social connections and self-care can actually contribute to the richness of one's writing, providing an abundance of experiences, emotions and perspectives.

Establishing specific writing goals and deadlines is crucial. Setting achievable milestones and taking time to develop your unique writing schedule and roadmap, ensures consistent progress without the overwhelm.

Books are dying

The mere thought of this gives me hives. Books will never, ever die. They are one of the most enduring forms of human expression. From ancient manuscripts to modern novels, they have been a vessel for ideas, stories and knowledge. And this will continue.

In fact, books are experiencing a resurgence thanks to eBooks and audiobooks. Readers can carry an entire library in their pockets or soak in the wisdom of authors from across the globe, through their headphones while on their morning commute.

The key is to find the right platform for your book and market the book effectively.

Only children's books sell well

You need only enter the homes of book lovers everywhere to know that this is bollocks. The key is to write a book that appeals to your target audience. Many books are extremely popular with all ages, such as the Harry Potter series. And the personal development space is booming.

I need to write my own book

Wrong!

Many people believe that to become an author they must sit down and painstakingly write every single word themselves. However, that's just one way to produce a book. In reality, there are several effective methods to bring your ideas to life and publish a book without doing all the writing yourself.

1. Speak and transcribe

If you're more comfortable speaking than writing, you can simply dictate your book. There are loads of tools and services available that can transcribe your spoken words into written text. This approach allows you to capture your natural voice and thoughts more fluidly and quickly.

2. Hire a ghostwriter

Ghostwriters are professional writers who specialise in capturing your voice, ideas, and style to create a book on your behalf. This option is particularly useful if you have the ideas but lack the time or writing skills to put them into words. My team and I offer ghostwriting services if you'd like to chat about this option!

So, what does it take to become an author? The answer is simple: dedication and hard work. If you are willing to put in the effort, you can achieve your dream of becoming an author. Follow the path laid out in this book, and you will have a great manuscript to put through the publishing process and skyrocket your business to new heights.

"

I am convinced that anyone can be a great writer ... if he can only ... tell the naked truth about himself and other people. That, a little technique with words and the willingness to bare heart, soul and body are really all it takes.

CLIVE BARNES

ENGLISH WRITER AND CRITIC

SECTION 2

LAYING THE FOUNDATIONS FOR YOUR BESTSELLER

CHAPTER 7

THE PERFECT TOPIC
Aligning Your Expertise with Audience Demand

Choosing the right topic for your book is a pivotal decision that sets the stage for everything that follows. It's where your deep expertise intersects with your audience's most pressing needs, creating fertile ground for your authority to grow and flourish.

This chapter guides you through the process of identifying that perfect topic, ensuring your book is both a showcase for your knowledge and a valuable resource for your readers.

In the entrepreneurial world where ideas are currency and knowledge is power, finding the right concept for your book can feel really scary and overwhelming. People tend to romanticise the idea of writing a book, but honestly, there's nothing romantic about it. It takes dedication and a willingness to keep putting one word in front of the other until you have a manuscript that you are satisfied will make an impact on the people who read it, and on the bottom line of your business.

The intersection of passion and demand

Begin by listing the areas within your field where you possess deep knowledge and genuine passion. Passion fuels perseverance, especially when faced with the tight timeline of a 28-day book-writing challenge.

However, expertise and passion alone are not enough. Your chosen topic must also meet a clear market demand. This is where the insights from your market research become invaluable (I'll teach you how to do this later), highlighting the areas where your audience seeks guidance, inspiration or solutions.

So how do you come up with your book concept? Here are a few ways:

Evaluating market gaps and trends

With a list of potential topics in hand, turn your attention to identifying gaps in the market. What questions are your potential readers asking that haven't yet been adequately answered? What emerging trends within your field are not yet covered in existing books?

Take the time to research the books your competitors have written and figure out how you can write something even better. Look in bookstores, libraries and online platforms to see what's available. Perhaps you'll discover a niche that hasn't been adequately explored or you may find an opportunity to offer a fresh take on a subject. Nobody, after all, can teach something the same way you can.

By positioning your book at the forefront of these trends or filling these gaps, you establish yourself as a thought leader and go-to authority.

Solve problems or answer questions

Books that provide solutions to common problems or answer pressing questions are always in demand. Think about the challenges people face in their daily lives or the knowledge gaps that exist in a particular field. Your book can be a valuable resource by providing practical advice, insights or answers.

Draw from personal experiences

Your own life experiences can be a rich source of material. Consider your unique journey, whether it's overcoming adversity, achieving personal goals or gaining expertise in a particular area. Sharing your experiences can not only be therapeutic but also inspire and educate others.

Conduct interviews and research

Engaging with experts and conducting thorough research can lead to groundbreaking book ideas. Seek out interviews with professionals in your chosen field or embark on investigative journalism to uncover untold stories. Your book could shed light on hidden truths, inspire change or provide a comprehensive overview of a complex topic.

Experiment with creative synthesis

Sometimes, the most innovative non-fiction books emerge from the fusion of seemingly unrelated ideas or disciplines. Experiment with cross-pollination, where you combine concepts from different fields to create something entirely new. This approach can lead to groundbreaking insights and fresh perspectives.

Reflect on current events and trends

Pay attention to current events and trends in society, science, technology and culture. These can be a springboard for exploring timely and relevant non-fiction topics. By analysing and contextualising contemporary issues, you can contribute to the ongoing conversation and provide valuable insights.

Assessing the scope of your topic

A common mistake in choosing a topic is either going too broad and making it difficult to cover subject matter in sufficient depth or too narrow and limiting your book's appeal. The trick is to strive for a balance.

Your topic should be specific enough to provide in-depth coverage, but broad enough to attract a wide range of readers within your target audience. This balance ensures that your book is accessible and provides value to your reader.

Here are some examples:

Example 1: Too Broad

Topic: How to Succeed in Business

- Issue: The subject is extremely broad, covering a wide range of industries, strategies, and skills.
- Consequence: The book might end up being a general overview without providing actionable insights or detailed guidance on any specific aspect of running a business.

Example 2: Too Broad

Topic: All About Startups

- Issue: Startups encompass numerous areas such as funding, marketing, product development, team building, scaling, and more. Each area has its own complexities and best practices.
- Consequence: The author might struggle to delve deeply into each topic, resulting in a book that lacks depth and fails to offer substantial value to aspiring entrepreneurs.

Example 3: Too Narrow

Topic: How to Start a Dog Walking Business in Small Towns

- Issue: While niche topics can be helpful, this one is overly specific, focusing on a single type of business in a specific setting.
- Consequence: The book's audience would be extremely limited, appealing only to a very small group of potential readers. This could lead to poor sales and limited reach.

Example 4: Too Narrow

Topic: Marketing Strategies for Vegan Cupcake Bakeries in Urban Areas

- Issue: This topic is very specific, targeting a narrow niche within a niche market.
- Consequence: The book's appeal is minimal, and it might struggle to find a broad audience, making it difficult to justify the investment of time and resources in writing and publishing it.

Balanced Example

Topic: The Lean Startup: How to Build a Successful Business with Minimal Resources

- Strength: This topic is focused yet broad enough to cover various aspects of starting and running a lean business, such as validating ideas, minimising waste, and maximising efficiency.
- Consequence: The book can attract a wide audience of aspiring entrepreneurs looking for practical advice on building a successful business with limited resources.

Balanced Example

Topic: From Idea to Launch: A Guide to Starting Your Own Tech Company

- Strength: This topic is specific enough to provide detailed guidance on the unique challenges of starting a tech company but broad enough to cover various stages of the entrepreneurial journey, from ideation to launch.
- Consequence: The book can offer valuable insights and practical advice, appealing to a broad audience of tech enthusiasts and aspiring entrepreneurs.

Balanced Example

Topic: Scaling Your Business: Strategies for Growth and Expansion

- Strength: This topic is focused on the critical stage of business growth and expansion, offering strategies and insights that can be applied to various industries.
- Consequence: The book can attract small business owners and entrepreneurs looking for practical advice on how to scale their businesses, providing enough depth to be informative and engaging.

Those examples focus on business but how about we also look at a different area such as health?

Example 1: Too Broad

Topic: All About Health

- Issue: Health is a vast field encompassing physical health, mental health, nutrition, exercise, preventative care, and more.
- Consequence: The book might end up being an unfocused overview, lacking the depth necessary to provide valuable insights or practical advice in any one area.

Example 2: Too Broad

Topic: Complete Guide to Medicine

- Issue: Medicine includes numerous specialities such as cardiology, neurology, oncology, paediatrics, and more, each with its own body of knowledge and practices.
- Consequence: The author might struggle to cover each speciality comprehensively, resulting in a superficial treatment of a complex field.

Example 3: Too Narrow

Topic: The Benefits of a Specific Herbal Supplement for Migraine Relief

- Issue: While niche topics can be valuable, this one is very narrow, focusing on a single supplement for a specific condition.
- Consequence: The book's audience would be extremely limited, appealing only to those interested in both herbal supplements and migraine relief. This could lead to poor sales and limited reach.

Example 4: Too Narrow

Topic: Yoga Poses for Finger Flexibility

- Issue: This topic is overly specific, targeting a very small aspect of yoga practice.
- Consequence: The book's appeal is minimal, and it might struggle to find a broad audience, making it difficult to justify the investment of time and resources in writing and publishing it.

Balanced Example

Topic: The Science of Nutrition: How to Eat for Optimal Health

- Strength: This topic is focused on nutrition but broad enough to cover various aspects such as macronutrients, micronutrients, dietary patterns, and the impact of nutrition on overall health.
- Consequence: The book can attract a wide audience interested in improving their health through nutrition, providing detailed, practical advice backed by scientific research.

Balanced Example

Topic: Mindfulness and Mental Health: Techniques for Stress Reduction and Emotional Well-Being

- Strength: This topic is specific to mindfulness practices but broad enough to cover various techniques and their benefits for mental health, including stress reduction and emotional well-being.
- Consequence: The book can offer valuable insights and practical advice, appealing to a broad audience interested in improving their mental health through mindfulness.

Balanced Example

Topic: Fitness for Life: Exercise Routines for Different Stages of Life

- Strength: This topic focuses on fitness but covers different stages of life, offering exercise routines and tips for children, adults, and seniors.
- Consequence: The book can attract a diverse audience, providing tailored advice for readers at different life stages, ensuring it is informative and engaging.

Distil the essence of your topic

By this stage, you should be ready to begin distilling the essence of your topic into a core message. What is the central idea? What problem are you addressing, or what insight are you providing?

Validating your topic with your audience

Before fully committing to your topic, validate it with your intended audience. Share your idea through your existing channels, whether that be a blog, email newsletter, social media or direct conversations. Gauge the response. Are people excited, intrigued or indifferent? Use this feedback to refine your topic, ensuring it resonates strongly with your ideal readers.

Seek feedback and brainstorm

Get yourself a book coach. Working with a book coach will help you get out of your head and see the forest for the trees. A coach can offer valuable feedback, suggest new angles or help you refine your concept.

I warn against sharing your ideas with too many friends and colleagues. This is not because they don't have any value to add, but because they are often too closely connected to you to help you really see the bigger picture.

That being said, if you have a close friend, family member or colleague who you intuitively know will be a valuable asset to you in writing your book, get them on board. I'm just saying, don't go involving every man and his dog.

Work smarter, not harder

As an entrepreneur, I bet you already have a whole bundle of valuable content stored on your Google Drive and other places. Work smarter and not harder, my friend. All of that content is excellent fodder for your book.

Have you created an online course? Turn your book into a lead-generator for that course. Have you written loads of articles and blog posts on a particular topic? Turn it into a book. Created a five-day challenge? Turn it into a book.

My team and I worked with Dr Carrie Spell-Hansson to turn her thesis and related articles into a book that catapulted her onto the speaking circuit and further helped to solidify her as the go-to authority in her field.

We turned my client Solomon's five-day challenge into a lead-generating book for his business, and the results have been incredible. He has more sign-ups to his platform than ever before.

Crafting a compelling book blurb

A book blurb is a brief summary or promotional description of your book, typically found on the back cover or inside flap of a book jacket. It is designed to capture the reader's interest and encapsulate the essence of your book's message. It should highlight your book's unique value and why it matters to your audience. A strong, clear blurb not only guides the writing of your book but is also a powerful tool in your marketing arsenal, capturing the interest of potential readers.

Here's a step-by-step guide along with examples to help you craft an effective book blurb:

1. Start with a hook

Begin with a surprising fact, a provocative question, or a compelling statement that highlights the importance of your book's topic.

Example:

"Did you know that over 60% of adults struggle with managing their time effectively?"

2. Introduce the main theme or concept

Clearly state the main topic or concept of your book and why it's important.

Example:

"In *Mastering Time: The Science of Productivity*, we delve into the psychology and strategies behind effective time management."

3. Outline the core benefits

Explain what the readers will gain from reading your book. This could be new insights, practical skills, or transformative knowledge.

Example:

"Through a combination of scientific research and practical advice, this book offers actionable techniques to help you prioritise tasks, reduce stress, and achieve your goals."

4. Highlight unique elements

Mention what makes your book stand out. It could be unique research, personal anecdotes, or a fresh perspective on a well-known topic.

Example:

"Unlike other productivity guides, *Mastering Time* integrates the latest findings from neuroscience with real-life case studies of successful individuals."

5. Conclude with a teaser

End with a call to action or thought-provoking question that leaves the reader wanting more.

Example:

"Are you ready to take control of your time and transform your life?"

Full example

Book statement for a non-fiction book on productivity:

"Did you know that over 60% of adults struggle with managing their time effectively? In *Mastering Time: The Science of Productivity*, we delve into the psychology and strategies behind effective time management. Through a combination of scientific research and practical advice, this book offers actionable techniques to help you prioritise tasks, reduce stress, and achieve your goals. Unlike other productivity guides, *Mastering Time* integrates the latest findings from neuroscience with real-life case studies of successful individuals. Are you ready to take control of your time and transform your life?"

Tips for writing your non-fiction book blurb

1. **Be concise:** Keep it short and to the point, ideally within 150-200 words.
2. **Focus on benefits:** Highlight what readers will gain from your book.
3. **Use clear language:** Avoid jargon and make your statement easily understandable.
4. **Know your audience:** Tailor your statement to appeal to your target readers.

Examples from different non-fiction genres

Self-help

"Are you tired of feeling overwhelmed and stressed in your daily life? In *Stress Less, Live More: A Holistic Guide to Well-Being*, wellness coach Calamity Calm offers a comprehensive approach to managing stress and enhancing your overall well-being. This transformative guide combines mindfulness techniques, nutrition advice, and personal stories, to provide a holistic blueprint for a healthier, happier life.

Through engaging exercises and real-life examples, *Stress Less, Live More* empowers you to take control of your stress levels and create lasting changes. Whether you're dealing with work-related stress, personal issues, or simply seeking a more balanced life, this book offers valuable tools and insights to help you thrive.

Are you ready to transform your life and embrace a new way of living? Start your journey to well-being with *Stress Less, Live More* and unlock the secrets to a stress-free, fulfilling life."

Health and wellness

"Did you know that small changes to your diet can lead to significant improvements in your health? In *The Power of Nutrition: Transform Your Life with Superfoods*, Dr. Eat Less Crap explores the incredible impact that nutrient-dense foods can have on your overall well-being. This comprehensive guide provides a deep dive into the science behind superfoods and offers practical tips for incorporating them into your daily routine.

In *The Power of Nutrition*, you'll discover the secrets to boosting your energy levels, enhancing your immune system, and achieving a healthier lifestyle. Through easy-to-understand explanations and evidence-based advice, Dr. Eat Less Crap breaks down the complex world of nutrition into actionable steps that anyone can follow. Whether you're looking to lose weight, manage chronic conditions, or simply feel better every day, this book offers a wealth of knowledge and tools to help you succeed.

Are you ready to take charge of your health and unlock the full potential of your body? Embark on a journey to wellness with *The Power of Nutrition* and discover the life-changing benefits of a superfood-rich diet."

Relationships

"Why do some relationships thrive while others falter? In *The Science of Love: Building Lasting Relationships*, relationship expert Dr. Cupid explores the key factors that contribute to strong, enduring partnerships. Drawing from decades of research in psychology and sociology, this book provides actionable insights and practical advice for nurturing intimacy, improving communication, and resolving conflicts.

Through compelling case studies and real-life examples: *The Science of Love* demystifies the complex dynamics of romantic relationships. Whether you're in a new relationship, navigating the challenges of a long-term partnership, or seeking to strengthen your bond, this book offers valuable tools to help you create a loving and resilient connection.

Discover the secrets to a fulfilling relationship and learn how to build a foundation of trust, respect, and mutual understanding. Are you ready to transform your love life?"

Book blurbs are used in various places, including:

- **Back cover:** The most common location for a blurb, where potential buyers often glance to get a quick idea of the book.
- **Inside flap:** In hardcover books, the blurb may appear on the inside front flap of the dust jacket.
- **Online retailers:** On websites like Amazon or Goodreads, blurbs are featured prominently on the book's sales page.
- **Publisher's website:** Publishers often include the blurb in the book's listing on their own website.
- **Marketing materials:** Blurbs may be used in promotional materials, such as brochures, press releases, or advertisements.

The book blurb is a critical marketing tool that plays a significant role in attracting readers and driving book sales.

The unique angle: standing out in a crowded market

To make your book truly stand out, you must find a unique angle or approach to your topic. This could be your unique method, a different combination of concepts, or personal stories and case studies that illustrate your points in a way no one else can.

Your unique angle is what will differentiate your book from others on similar topics, making it a must-read within your industry.

Here are **three crucial steps** for developing and validating your unique book angle:

1. Understand what people are searching for on Amazon:

Discover search trends:

1.   Open Google Chrome in incognito mode.
2.   Navigate to Amazon.com.
3.   Select "Kindle" as the category.
4.   Begin typing your book ideas into the search bar. Amazon will automatically show you suggestions based on popular searches.

Refine your ideas: Use these suggestions to narrow down your book ideas or explore new topics.

Use the handy spreadsheet included at the end of this chapter to write down all the book names that grab your attention and which you'd like to model. Keep filling out this spreadsheet so you can keep your research organised!

2. Determine if people will pay for your book idea:

Assess market demand:

1. Enter your book idea into the Amazon search bar and perform a search.
2. Review the books that appear in the results.
3. Click on each book, scroll down, and note the "Amazon Best Sellers Rank" (ABSR).

Evaluate sales potential:

- The ABSR ranges from 1 to 4.8 million, with 1 being the best. Books with a lower ABSR (closer to 1) indicate higher sales.
- If books related to your idea have a low ABSR, it suggests a strong market demand and a willingness to pay.

3. Assess competition in your chosen topic:

Analyse competitor data:

- Look at the ABSR for competing books. If most ranks are below 10,000, the competition is high.

Identify opportunities:

- Don't be discouraged by competition. If existing books have poor titles or covers and you believe you can do better, there's a chance to stand out.
- Amazon favours newer books. Check the publication dates; out-dated books mean less recent competition, which can present an opportunity for your new book.

Ideally, working out the topic for your book will incorporate one or more of these pathways:

If you've ever helped someone achieve something or had an impact on another person for the better, then you already have the knowledge you need to write a book. Write about that process.

If you have a passion that you can't stop telling people about, then you already have your book idea. Write about that.

If you are committed to doing the work of sitting your butt down, parking your perfectionism and self-doubt at the door, putting one word in front of the other and getting it done, then you can write a book.

The entire contents of this book are me sharing why I love books so much, how they have been proven to grow businesses and change lives, and the exact method my team and I use to serve our global client base of international bestselling author entrepreneurs. Out of the above pathways for the theme of this book, I created my own cocktail of:

- My passions
- A recognition that there was a gap in the market
- Solving problems and answering questions
- Drawing on my personal experiences
- Working smarter, not harder

Selecting the perfect topic for your book is a strategic process that requires a delicate balance between your expertise, market demand and a unique angle. By carefully navigating this process, you ensure your book not only exemplifies your authority, but also meets a real need within your target audience, setting the foundation for the book's success.

Your chosen topic is not just the subject of your book. It's the vehicle through which you will connect with readers, build your brand and drive your business forward.

To help you with implementing this chapter I created three additional book bonuses:

- ✓ Crafting Your Hero's Story Training which will help you develop a compelling story thread for your book based on your own personal journey.
- ✓ The Million Dollar Book Concept Masterclass to guide you in developing a book concept that will be highly successful and marketable.
- ✓ Live BTS 1-on-1 Book Concept Creation Coaching Call Recording allowing you to observe the coaching process and gain valuable tips, techniques and real-world examples of how to refine and enhance your own book concept.

You can access these bonus resources by scanning the QR code below:

Book topic discovery worksheet

Objective: To identify the perfect topic for your book.

Grab a piece of paper to brainstorm some potential hooks for your book. It doesn't have to be perfect yet. Use this stage of the journey to get creative and have fun.

Section 1: Passion and Expertise

1. **Be yourself:** If you could write about anything, without any rules or worrying about what others would think, what would you write about?
2. **Find your passion:** What are you most passionate about in your business? Write down areas within your field where you possess deep knowledge and genuine passion.
3. **Passion meets perseverance:** How do your interests fuel your willingness to commit to the writing process? Provide examples.

Section 2: Market Demand and Trends

1. **Conduct market research:** Note down methods you will use to understand your audience's needs (eg, surveys, social media engagement, calls). Then do it.
2. **Identify gaps and trends:** Based on your research, list potential topics that address unanswered questions or emerging trends in your field.
3. **Evaluate competition:** Review what existing books cover topics similar to yours and brainstorm how your book could offer something better or different.

Section 3: Problem-Solving and Unique Experiences

1. **Solve a problem:** What are the top three problems you solve for your clients?
2. **Common questions:** What are the most common questions you get asked to answer all the time, either from your clients or on podcasts, in the media, etc.?
3. **Personal journey:** How can your personal experiences inform your book topic? List significant experiences that could be relevant.

Section 4: Research and Creative Synthesis

1. **Plan for interviews/research:** Outline who you could interview or what research could be done to find unique insights for your book.
2. **Creative combination:** Think of ways to blend different disciplines or ideas for a fresh perspective. List any innovative combinations.

Section 5: Current Events and Scope

1. **Current events and relevance:** How can current events or societal trends influence your book topic? Note down ideas.
2. **Assessing topic scope:** Ensure your topic isn't too broad or too narrow. Define the scope of your intended topic.

Section 6: Audience Validation and Unique Angle

1. **Validate with audience:** Describe how you will share your idea with your audience and gather feedback.
2. **Find your unique angle:** What makes your approach unique? List ideas that could differentiate your book in the market.

Section 7: Feedback, Brainstorming and Content Use

1. **Seek feedback:** Approach your chosen book coach or one or more trusted individuals to gather feedback on your topic idea.
2. **Use existing content:** Make an inventory of existing content (eg, courses, articles) that could be repurposed for your book.

Section 8: Crafting Your Book Statement

1. **Book statement draft:** Write a compelling statement that encapsulates your book's unique value and message.

Reflection and Action Plan:

- From the above sections, identify the most compelling topics that align with your expertise, passion and market demand.
- Select the top three topics and outline a brief action plan for further exploration or validation for each. Who knows – you may end up writing all three books, but we must start with one first!
- Decide on a timeline for each step in your action plan to maintain momentum in your book topic discovery process.

You can do this exercise on a piece of paper, or if you'd like to download a digital version of this worksheet, scan the QR code below:

Unique Angle Research

Title	Subtitle	URL	Best-seller status – yes/no?	Best-seller ranking	Categories ranking for	Publication date	Number of pages

You can do this exercise on a piece of paper, or if you'd like to download a digital version of this spreadsheet, scan the QR code below:

Topic brainstorm session

Objective: To come up with some topics for your book.

Grab a piece of paper to brainstorm some potential topics for your book. It doesn't have to be perfect yet. Use what you have discovered so far to help you craft some potential topics.

_____

_____

_____

_____

_____

_____

_____

_____

_____

_____

You can do this exercise on a piece of paper, or if you'd like to download a digital version of this spreadsheet, scan the QR code below:

"

This is how you do it: you sit down at the keyboard and you put one word after another until it's done. It's that easy, and that hard.

NEIL GAIMAN

AUTHOR

CHAPTER 8

YOUR IDEAL READER

The cornerstone of any successful book, particularly one aimed at establishing authority and driving marketing success, is a profound understanding of its intended audience. It's not about you. It never is when it comes to writing. Sure, it starts with your voice in your head and on the page, but if you want readers to stick around for more than a sentence or two, you need to forget about yourself and focus on them instead.

Who are your ideal readers? What do they like? What are their hopes and fears? Once you know the answers to these questions, you can start writing for them – and that's when the magic happens. This chapter delves into the critical process of market research, a step that transforms guesswork into strategy, ensuring your book resonates deeply with your readers, addressing with precision their needs, desires and challenges.

Your ideal readers are those who will fall in love with you and your work. These are the ones who will recommend your book to their friends and leave glowing reviews on Amazon. But to get them there, you have to give them what they want – and that means writing for them not for yourself. It's a very similar process to working out your ideal client avatar for business, but in this case, it's your ideal reader avatar (IRA). You will most likely find that, in this case, they are one and the same.

Take the time to know who they are. This seems like a no-brainer, but you'd be surprised how many people try to write without a clear picture of who their target audience is. If you don't know who you're writing for, it's impossible to write something that will resonate with them.

Doing your research is something you just cannot skip if you want your book and your business to be a success. Trust me, I tried that short-cut and it fell flatter than a pancake dropped from a great height. At the end of this chapter, I give you some questions to consider which will help you define your IRA. Do not skip this part unless you are 100 percent confident you have already nailed your ideal client and, therefore, your IRA.

The why and how of market research

Market research is not just about identifying who your audience is. It's about understanding that audience. This understanding forms the foundation on which your book is built, ensuring it speaks directly to the hearts and minds of your readers, solving their problems and enriching their lives or businesses.

Begin with the basics: reader demographic information such as age, gender, profession and location. Then, delve deeper into their psychographics – values, interests, challenges and aspirations. Tools like surveys, social media analytics and interviews are invaluable in gathering this information.

The goal is to paint a detailed picture of your ideal reader, a persona that you will keep in mind throughout the writing process.

Analysing competing titles

Part of understanding your audience involves knowing what other resources they are turning to for information. Analyse competing titles within your niches. What topics are they covering? What questions are left unanswered? What do readers appreciate about these books and what do they feel is lacking?

This information, often found in book reviews and on reader forums, can highlight gaps in the market your book can fill. Additionally, you can refer back to Chapter 7 on exactly how to find which books you would be competing with.

Engaging with your audience

Direct engagement with potential readers offers invaluable insights into their needs and preferences. Participate in online forums, attend industry conferences or host webinars to discuss topics related to your book.

These interactions not only inform your content strategy they also build anticipation and a sense of community around your upcoming book.

Utilising feedback loops

Feedback is a crucial component of effective market research. Share your book's outline or key concepts with a segment of your target audience and get the feedback. This could be through one-on-one interviews, focus groups or social media polls.

Pay close attention to the language they use when discussing their challenges and aspirations. Incorporating their words and phrases into your book can significantly increase engagement and how your book resonates with your readers.

Analysing data to inform your strategy

With data in hand, the next step is analysis. (It can be fun, I promise.) Look for patterns and trends in the information you've gathered. What are the most pressing problems your ideal readers face? What solutions are they seeking? This exploration will guide not only the content of your book but also how you position the book in the market.

Market research is not a step to be skipped or taken lightly. It's an investment in the success of your book and, by extension, your business.

Picture your ideal readers as close friends you haven't yet met. You want to impress them, make them laugh and maybe even bring a tear to their eye. You wouldn't start a conversation with these hypothetical friends by rambling on about your day or your latest accomplishments, right? No, you'd dive into topics that resonate with them, things that make them nod in agreement or lean in with interest.

That's exactly how you should approach your writing. Imagine your ideal readers sitting across from you, a cup of coffee in hand, ready to be entertained or enlightened. What stories would captivate them? What insights would make them think, 'Wow, this person really gets me'?

Think about it like a dinner party. You wouldn't serve a meal without considering your guests' tastes. Similarly, your writing is a feast for your readers, and you want them to leave the table satisfied, wanting more. So, as you put pen to paper (or fingers to keyboard), keep those imaginary friends in mind. What kind of language would they appreciate? What tone would resonate with them? Adjust your writing style accordingly.

It's not about being a people-pleaser. It's about establishing a connection. Remember, your ideal readers are on a journey and you're their guide. You want them to feel seen, heard and understood. This means addressing their questions, concerns and curiosities. If they've picked up your book, they're investing their time in you. Respect that investment by making it worth their while.

And don't forget the element of surprise. Just like any good friends, your ideal readers love a plot twist. Keep them guessing, throw in unexpected turns and don't be afraid to challenge assumptions. Your writing should be a delightful roller-coaster, not a predictable stroll in the park.

Think about your favourite non-fiction books. What made them stand out? It's likely that the author spoke to you on a personal level, weaving a narrative that felt tailor-made for your interests and sensibilities. Strive to create that same connection for your readers.

Remember, it's not about you. It's about those imaginary friends across the table, eagerly awaiting the next sentence, the next chapter. When you write for your ideal readers, you're giving them something special that they can't find anywhere else. You're creating a connection that will keep your readers coming back for more, and that's what it's all about.

By taking the time to understand your audience's needs, desires and challenges, you ensure your book is not just another item on a shelf but a valuable resource that establishes your authority, builds trust and drives business growth.

So, don't be afraid to put yourself out there and write for the people who matter most to you. It'll be worth it in the end.

"

Approach each customer with the idea of helping him or her solve a problem or achieve a goal, not of selling a product or service.

BRIAN TRACY

MOTIVATIONAL SPEAKER AND
SELF-DEVELOPMENT AUTHOR

Defining your ideal reader avatar (IRA)

Objective: To dive deeply into really getting to know the people you want to read your book.

Important reminder: This requires actual research and not guesswork!

1. Do they identify as male, female or other?
2. What is their age range?
3. Are they married, in a relationship, single, divorced or other?
4. What is their income?
5. Do they have children?
6. Where do they live?
7. What is their educational background?
8. What kind of books do they like to read?
9. Where are they looking for solutions (online, offline, brochures, etc.)?
10. Where are they hanging out?
11. What are their interests?
12. How do they communicate (e.g. phone, email, text, etc.)?
13. What do they do in their spare time?
14. What do they do for work?
15. What keeps them awake at night?
16. Before reading your book they feel...?
17. What do they find frustrating?
18. What do they find frustrating that they would never voice out loud?

19. What do they think is the problem?

20. What do they think they need to solve their problem?

21. What do they actually need? (Note: this is often different to what someone thinks they need.)

22. What are some of the key phrases they use to describe their problem?

23. They know that if they don't find a solution to their problem they will …

24. What is important to them?

25. They will find your book valuable if …

26. How do they speak in everyday life (e.g. do they swear, like a play on words, use slang, have a sense of humour, etc.)?

27. Do they like lots of visual cues or are they more inclined to words?

28. Do they like completing exercises or prefer gathering knowledge?

29. Who are the successful authors in your genre, and who is their audience?

I encourage you to take time to reflect on each question and use the answers to create a clear profile of your target audience. This understanding will not only shape your writing style and content, but also help in marketing the book effectively.

You can do this exercise on a piece of paper, or if you'd like to download a digital version of this worksheet, scan the QR code below:

CHAPTER 9

REELING THEM IN
The Art of Book Hooks

All right, buckle up! We're diving into the exhilarating world of book hooks. If you've ever wondered why some books grab your attention from the first page and refuse to let go, it's likely the author has mastered the art of the hook.

What's a book hook anyway?

Think of a book hook as literary bait, the irresistible lure that makes readers take the plunge into your world. It's that magnetic force that prompts them to pick up your book and say, 'Just one more chapter.' A book hook is your chance to make a lasting first impression, to captivate and to intrigue.

In simpler terms, a book hook is a compelling, concise statement that sparks curiosity and sets the tone for your entire masterpiece. It's the literary equivalent of a movie trailer, but instead of showcasing explosions and heart-pounding music, it promises an intellectual, emotional and transformative journey.

The placement of a book hook is crucial, and it typically appears in the opening lines or paragraphs. It should also appear on the back cover and, ideally, in the title or subtitle of your book in some form.

Why hooks matter

Why are hooks crucial? In a world flooded with books, your potential readers are playing a constant game of literary speed dating. A captivating hook is your way of saying, 'Pick me! I'm worth your time. I hold the solution to your problem.' It's the difference between your book gathering dust on the shelf or becoming a dog-eared favourite that gets recommended again and again – and again.

A well-crafted hook not only entices readers, but also provides a roadmap for your writing. It keeps you focused and ensures that every chapter contributes to the overall narrative. It's not just about grabbing attention – it's about holding it.

Sell the tools

It's crucial to recognise that individuals aren't looking to purchase more information – free information is everywhere these days. Buyers want to invest in tools and solutions that promise to help them achieve a certain goal or solve a specific problem.

If your book offers a glut of information, it won't reach its full sales potential and certainly won't transform readers into clients, and a book that only contains information will leave some readers feeling disappointed when they realise they paid for something they could have accessed free online.

For your book to gain a special place on bookshelves around the world, you need to ensure that what you are giving your readers is a system, a framework and your experience and wisdom to help its readers achieve meaningful goals. All of this gets communicated in your book hook.

Let's look at a couple of examples.

I just bought Alex Hormozi's new book titled *$100M Leads – How to Get Strangers to Want to Buy Your Stuff*. This title tells me that I am buying a system of some sort that will help me a) potentially generate $100M worth of leads and b) solve the entrepreneurial issue of turning cold leads into clients.

Additionally, Alex has also evoked feelings of excitement, hope and curiosity about what he is offering. A total winning book title and hook! Imagine if he had called the book something like *How to Get More Clients for Your Business*. Much less enticing, right?

How about Patrick Bet-David's book, *Your Next Five Moves – Master the Art of Business Strategy*. The title clearly indicates that what the reader is getting is a system – a set of step-by-step instructions, the exact five steps needed for that reader to move his or her business forward in a strategic way. Now, he could have also called the book *Five Strategic Business Moves* – much less impact, don't you think?

Fundamentally, people want to learn from others who have 'figured it out', be it lead generation, business strategy or life in general. Readers don't want lectures or an influx of facts. Readers want someone who can say, 'Have this problem? Here's how I solved it, and here's how you can, too.' Nothing conveys 'I figured it out' more effectively than a hook built around a framework. Essentially, you're selling your solution, your unique selling point, your disruptive idea.

Crafting your own hook

Now, the million-dollar (quite literally) question: How do you concoct a hook that's as gripping as a suspense thriller or the latest dance trend on TikTok?

1. Identify the core message

Start by pinpointing the essence of your book. What's the big idea? What problem are you solving or what insight are you offering? Your hook should be a sneak peek into this core message.

2. Tap into emotions

Don't just appeal to the intellect, engage the heart. Whether it's curiosity, hope or excitement, evoke emotions that resonate with your readers. Make them feel something, and you've got them hooked.

3. Be specific and concise

Avoid vague generalities. Be specific about what makes your book unique. Use vivid language but keep it concise. A hook is not the time for an information dump. It's a teaser, a taste that leaves them hungry for more.

4. Create intrigue

Leave room for questions. A good hook doesn't reveal everything. Instead, it hints, teases and invites readers to unravel the mysteries within your pages. Don't give it all away on the first date!

5. Test and refine

Just like a chef perfecting a recipe, don't be afraid to experiment. Test your hook on friends, family or clients. Pay attention to their reactions and be willing to refine your hook until it sings.

Putting it all together

If readers are the fish and the ocean is vast, what are you putting on your line to catch them? A well-crafted hook is your best shot at reeling them in. Remember, the better the hook, the larger the catch.

Crafting a compelling hook is an art that takes practice, so don't be discouraged if it doesn't come to you immediately. Experiment, revise and, most importantly, have fun with it. Your book deserves a hook that's as captivating as the journey it promises. Now go ahead, cast that line. Let the world get hooked on your words.

"

Creative non-fiction writers do not make things up; they make ideas and information that already exist more interesting and often more accessible.

LEE GUTKIND

WRITER AND SPEAKER

Harnessing your book hook

Objective: To craft a hook that lands your readers and doesn't let them go until they reach the final page and then become a loyal fan jumping to buy your stuff.

1. What is the core problem or challenge that your book addresses? This helps to identify the central theme or issue.

2. Who is your target audience, and what are their key pain points or desires? Understanding your audience's needs and interests will help you craft the hook to resonate with them.

3. What unique perspective or solution does your book offer? Highlight distinctive aspects that set it apart from others in the same genre or topic.

4. What emotions do you want your readers to experience while reading your book? Consider the emotional impact you want to have, whether it's inspiration, empowerment, curiosity or something else.

5. Can you distil the essence of your book into a concise, memorable statement or tagline? Crafting a succinct and special message can make your book more memorable and shareable.

6. What questions or problems will your book answer or solve for the reader? Clearly articulate the value proposition by highlighting the practical benefits the reader will gain.

7. How can you create a sense of urgency or curiosity in your hook? Consider incorporating elements that make readers feel compelled to learn more or take immediate action.

8. What systems and frameworks have you developed or can you develop around what you offer?

9. Brainstorm some book hooks. Remember to keep your hook clear, concise and focused on the most compelling aspects of your book.

You can do this exercise on a piece of paper, or if you'd like to download a digital version of this worksheet, scan the QR code below:

Book hook brainstorm session

Objective: To come up with some hooks for your book.

Grab a piece of paper to brainstorm some potential hooks for your book. It doesn't have to be perfect yet. Use this stage of the journey to get creative and have fun!

_____

_____

_____

_____

_____

_____

_____

_____

_____

_____

You can do this exercise on a piece of paper, or if you'd like to download a digital version of this worksheet, scan the QR code below:

CHAPTER 10

CHOOSING A TITLE FOR YOUR BOOK

Choosing the right title for your book is like finding the perfect seasoning for a dish. It makes all the difference. You want to craft a title that not only grabs attention but encapsulates the essence of your book. So how do we do that?

The hook: reeling them in

Here it is again, that all important hook!

Think of your title as the bait on your hook – it needs to be enticing enough to lure your readers. A good title sparks curiosity and invites potential readers to explore the contents. It's the first impression, the opening that sets the tone. Make it count.

Consider your target audience. What words or phrases resonate? What would catch the eye? Imagine scanning a bookstore or scrolling through an online catalogue. What title would make you stop and say, 'I need to know more about this?' (Remember we covered hooks in Chapter 9.)

Just to be clear though, a book hook, title and subtitle are different things. Here's how the three work together:

1. Title: The main name of the book, designed to grab attention and give a sense of what the book is about.
2. Subtitle: A secondary title that provides additional detail or context about the book's content, making the subject matter clearer.
3. Hook: A brief, compelling statement used to attract interest and curiosity, often used in marketing materials.

All three elements should, in some way, hook the reader and entice them to want to know more about your book.

Clarity trumps cleverness

While it's tempting to showcase your wit and creativity, clarity should be your guiding light when coming up with a title. A title that's too clever for its own good might leave potential readers scratching their heads instead of reaching for your book.

Your title should offer a glimpse into the subject matter. Imagine someone scanning your title and immediately grasping the general idea of what your book is about. It's the balance between intrigue and straightforwardness.

More often than not, a simpler title is the winner. Your title needs to label exactly what is in the book, not be up for a humour award. I came up with all sorts of amazingly creative titles for this book but in the end, the title does what it says on the tin, so to speak.

Keywords and search engine optimisation

In this digital age, being discovered is key. Readers often turn to search engines and online retailers to find books. Incorporating relevant keywords in your title can significantly boost your book's visibility.

Think about the words or phrases someone might type into a search engine when looking for a book like yours. Ensure those keywords find a comfortable home in your title, helping your book surface in relevant searches.

Here are some practical steps to help you research and select keywords for your book:

1 Identify your target audience	Clearly define your target audience. Who are the readers you want to attract? Knowing your audience will guide your keyword selection. (Refer back to Chapter 8 if you skipped that bit.)
2 Competitor analysis	Examine the titles of books similar to yours. What keywords do successful books in your genre or niche use? Analyse bestsellers and identify those with a similar level of exposure you would like for your book.
3 Google Keyword Planner	Leverage tools like Google Keyword Planner to research popular search terms related to your book's genre or subject matter. This tool provides insights into the average monthly search volume for specific keywords, helping you identify high-impact terms.

4 Amazon keyword research	Amazon is a major platform for book sales, so explore the Amazon search bar. Begin typing keywords related to your book and take note of the suggestions that appear. These autocomplete suggestions can provide valuable insights into what readers are searching for.
5 Use synonyms and variations	Don't limit yourself to a narrow set of keywords. Consider synonyms and variations of terms that might be relevant. This broadens the scope of potential search queries that could lead readers to your book.
6 Reader surveys and feedback	Engage with potential readers through surveys or seek feedback from beta readers. Ask about the words or phrases that come to mind when thinking about your book's topic. This can provide unique insights and uncover keywords you might not have considered.
7 Google Trends	Explore Google Trends to identify keywords that are trending or maintain consistent popularity over time. This can help you stay relevant and tap into topics that are capturing readers' interest.

Test the waters: feedback matters

Before you etch your title in stone, gather feedback from trusted friends, colleagues or beta readers. Present a few title options and gauge their reactions. Do they get it? Which one piques their interest the most? Honest feedback is a valuable compass, guiding you towards the title that resonates best.

The evergreen factor

While it's essential to capture the trend, consider the longevity of your title. Will it stand the test of time or does it risk becoming outdated? Aim for a title that can remain relevant and intriguing, even as the years roll by.

The power of subtitles

Don't underestimate the power of a subtitle. If your main title is the bait, think of the subtitle as the additional flavour that provides more context. It provides an opportunity to elaborate on the promise made by the title and offer a compelling reason for readers to delve deeper.

Think of it as a conversation starter. The main title is like introducing yourself at a party – being concise and to the point – the subtitle is where you start to share the juicy details. It's the opportunity to weave a narrative to set the stage for the reader. You're not just selling a book; you're inviting someone to join you on a journey.

Let's not forget the power of context. The main title might give you a general idea, but the subtitle is the decoder ring that helps you interpret the hidden messages.

It's the difference between *Atomic Habits* and *Atomic Habits: An Easy & Proven Way to Build Good Habits & Break Bad Ones*, the book by James Clear that has sold well over a million copies. Or *12 Months to $1 Million* and *12 Months to $1 Million: How to Pick a Winning Product, Build a Real Business, and Become a Seven-Figure Entrepreneur* by Ryan Daniel Moran.

The subtitle is like a compass, guiding you towards the specific direction of the adventure that awaits.

Trust your gut, but be willing to change

Ultimately, choosing a title is a blend of art and intuition. Trust your instincts but be open to refinement. You might find that your initial title, while poetic, needs a practical tweak to reach its full potential. I often find that I start writing a book with a specific title in mind but only when it's finished do I come up with the final title.

In this context, the name of the destination may reveal itself at the end of your writing journey.

Remember, your title is the ambassador of your book to the world. It deserves careful consideration and a dash of creativity. So, go ahead and experiment, and enjoy the process of birthing the perfect title for your non-fiction gem.

To help with implementing this chapter I have created two additional book bonuses:

- ✓ The Ultimate Bestselling Book Title Power Word Glossary to help you craft a book title that grabs attention and attracts readers.
- ✓ Write Your Book Title and Tagline Step-by-Step Training which provides a detailed, guided process for crafting compelling book titles and taglines, ensuring that your book's first impression is powerful and engaging.

You can access these bonus resources by scanning the QR code below:

"

Your book title is prime

sales real estate.

TARRYN REEVES

AUTHOR, PUBLISHER AND SPEAKER

Title brainstorm session

Objective: To come up with some titles and subtitles for your book.

Grab a piece of paper to brainstorm some potential titles and subtitles for your book. It doesn't have to be perfect yet. Use this stage of the journey to bring forth the creative juices of your forthcoming masterpiece.

_____

_____

_____

_____

_____

_____

_____

_____

You can do this exercise on a piece of paper, or if you'd like to download a digital version of this worksheet, scan the QR code below:

CHAPTER 11

CRAFTING A BESTSELLER
The Recipe for Turning Readers into Clients

I promised to keep it real, so here it is.

If you write a book and then choose to hit the Publish button and sit back, waiting for leads, clients and a return on your investment to roll in, you will be rolling in misery instead of money.

On your journey to writing and publishing your book, you may hear many horror stories from naive entrepreneurs who tried to grow their business with a book and have been sadly disappointed with their results.

It's not that the books these people wrote suck. It's just that they didn't follow the process through to the end. In short, they did it the wrong way. But you're not going to do that. I won't let you. You're going to follow the steps laid out in this book, see a return on your investment, scale your business, free up your time and become a raving fan of using books to grow businesses.

When writing your book, you must keep the notion of turning readers into paying clients at the forefront of your mind. Many authors struggle with this aspect of their business, but it doesn't have to be difficult. By providing an amazing reader experience, you can create a connection with your audience that will encourage readers to return for more, both on and off the pages.

Write a great book

So, how do you create an amazing reader experience? First and foremost, it starts with writing a great book. Your book has to deliver what the blurb on the back promises, be easy to read, flow smoothly, make the reader feel, and have a professional quality cover design and internal layout.

But that's not all. You also need a consistent social media presence that makes it easy for readers to connect with you and learn more about your work. Additionally, offering free content, such as blog posts or newsletter sign-ups, can give readers a taste of what you have to offer and help build trust between you and your audience.

Give it away

I also suggest that you try to include several downloadable free resources throughout your book, so that the reader has a chance to come off the page and into your digital world. You don't want them to just read the book and say, 'That was nice', and then put it on their bookshelf to gather dust. No! We want them to move, to take action, to take a step closer to you.

Once you have finished writing your chapters, go through each one and see if you have already created something or can create something to encourage your readers to take action and get results. Then simply add the link, or QR code (some helpful things did come out of Covid), to the end of your chapter, ensuring that it still flows and is not just some random link hanging on the end.

Just ask

You also want to be sure to include a strong call to action in the conclusion section of your book. Take every opportunity to invite the reader to connect more. As long as it feels natural and flows smoothly, then do it.

Be a human

Finally, don't forget the power of personal connection. If you can meet your readers in person at events or signings, or even just through social media interaction, you'll be much more likely to turn them into paying clients who will support your work for years.

So, there you have it. By following these simple tips, you can create an amazing reader experience that will turn your readers into paying clients.

By now, I'm sure you understand that a book is the best way to simplify your marketing, establish yourself as the authority in your space and have warm clients rolling in regularly, eager to buy your stuff.

The next step is to ensure that your book is not only a literary masterpiece but also a lucrative venture. Your book needs nine essential ingredients to become a bestseller and, more importantly, to turn those readers into loyal paying clients.

Nine essential ingredients for a bestselling book

1. Compelling, concise content is non-negotiable

First things first – your book needs to be like a magnetic force that draws readers in and refuses to let go. Engaging, relevant and valuable content is the lifeblood of your success. Your words must resonate with your target audience.

Take the time to understand the readers' pain points, dreams and desires, and weave your story around them. Make the readers feel their pain, allow them to connect with you by letting the essence of you loose on the pages, and – most importantly – make your readers think.

Your book doesn't need to be as long as *The Lord of The Rings* trilogy to be a success, either. Short and sweet (like me!) does the trick in an age where time is more valuable than gold.

The advantage of a concise book lies in its ability to reveal all without holding back any secrets. It's not like a webinar (remember when they told us we would only be successful if we ran a billion webinars a quarter? – sigh) or a video sales letter, where only a glimpse is offered. Lay it all out – tell your story, teach your method, bare it all.

When writing your book, the goal is to cram it with valuable information within the beginning 25% of your book. The first point to consider is to keep the content actionable. Can the reader implement what you're teaching? Are there exercises to enhance their life based on the information provided?

In addition, try to make whatever it is you are teaching memorable. Can you create an acronym for a key idea or develop step-by-step frameworks, instructions and processes? The essence is to make accessing the benefits of your guidance as simple as possible.

2. A killer hook and irresistible title

Your book's cover might be the first thing that catches a reader's eye, but it's the title and hook that make them pick it up. Craft a title that is not only catchy but also reflects the essence of your book. The hook – the first few pages – should be so compelling that readers can't help but keep turning the pages. It's like the trailer to a blockbuster movie. Make it impossible to resist.

3. Know your audience like the back of your hand

One size does not fit all when it comes to books. Understand your target audience and tailor your content to meet your readers' specific needs. For example, if you're writing for young professionals, your tone and examples should resonate with that demographic. Knowing your audience is not just about writing for them, it's about creating a connection that goes beyond the pages.

4. Cover those FAQs

Convert the questions your ideal clients ask you most frequently into chapters in your book. The most effective short books are designed to serve the reader, addressing their questions in a way that gives them confidence in what they are discovering.

Keep in mind that confused people don't buy, so your book's key goal should be to maximise clarity around what you are teaching and, ultimately, what you are offering for sale.

5. Build a brand, not just a book

Your book is not just a standalone product, it's a part of your personal or professional brand. Consistency is key. From your author biography to your online presence, everything should align with the image you want to portray. A cohesive brand builds trust, and trust is what turns readers into clients.

6. Strategic marketing and promotion

Even the most fantastic book won't sell itself. I see so many people throw their book on Amazon, having done the publication on the cheap, then sit back and expect the sales and moola to start rolling in.

I can tell you they are sadly disappointed. Each and every one of them. You must develop a robust marketing strategy that includes a strong online presence, social media campaigns and perhaps even some old-fashioned book signings (gosh, I love those!). Leverage every tool at your disposal to create buzz around your book. Remember, it's not just about selling a book, it's about selling an experience.

7. Incentivise your readers to take action

Your book is not the end goal – it's the gateway. Create opportunities for your readers to take the next step. Whether it's through exclusive content, workshops or personalised consultations, offer something that adds value and encourages them to become paying clients. Make them feel like they're part of an exclusive club with benefits.

8. Leverage the power of reviews and testimonials

Word of mouth is a powerful marketing tool. Encourage your readers to leave reviews and testimonials. Positive reviews build credibility and trust. Potential clients are more likely to take the plunge when they see others praising your work.

9. Stay engaged: the conversation continues

As previously mentioned, the book is just the beginning of the conversation. Stay engaged with your readers through social media, newsletters and events. Keep the momentum going by discussing the themes of your book, sharing behind-the-scenes insights and fostering a sense of community among your readers. The more engaged they are, the more likely they are to become long-term clients.

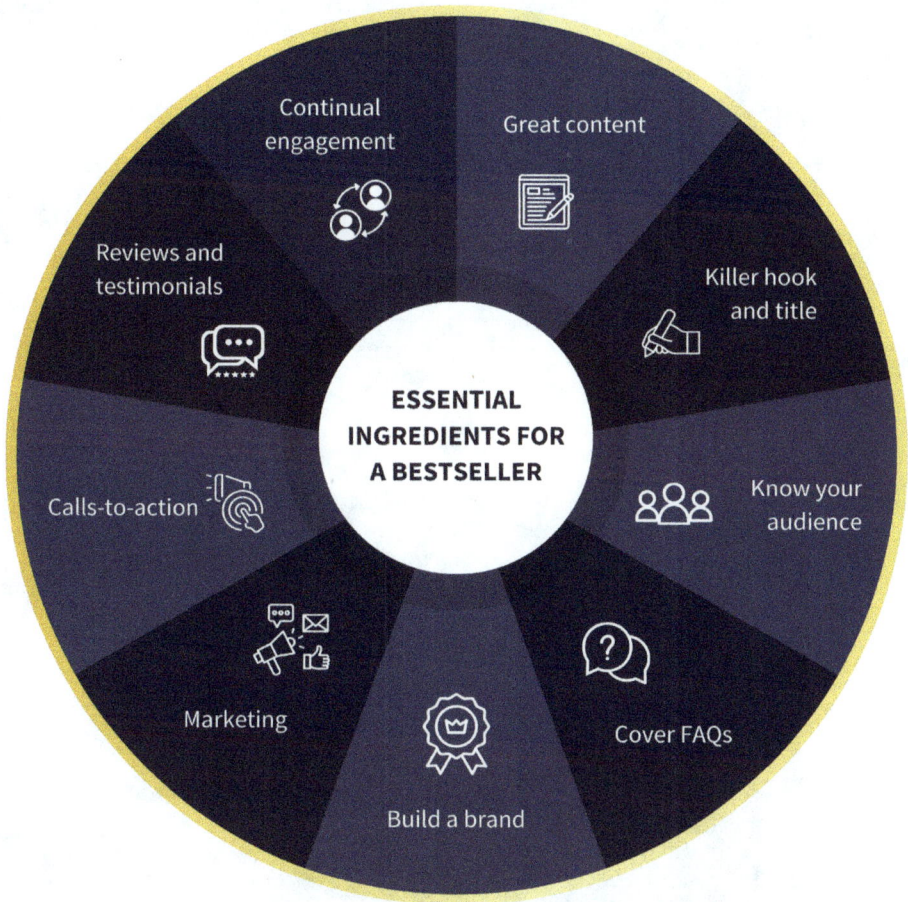

Figure 8: Essential ingredients for a bestselling book

Turning readers into paying clients is not just about selling a book, it's about selling an experience and building a relationship. We discuss many of these concepts further on in this book, but I have created a handy checklist for you to ensure that you cover all bases as you begin to craft your bestseller.

"

Reading is a conversation. All books talk. But a good book listens as well.

MARK HADDON

ENGLISH NOVELIST

The Bestseller Ingredient List

Objective: To ensure you action each of the nine ingredients that will make your book a bestseller.

- Compelling, concise content
- A killer hook
- An irresistible title
- Get to know your ideal reader
- Build a brand
- Marketing and promotional plan
- Incentivise the reader to take action
- Reviews and testimonials
- Engagement

If you'd like to download a digital version of this checklist, scan the QR code below:

CHAPTER 12

THE BLUEPRINT
Planning Your Authority Book

Embarking on the journey to write a book within 28 days that positions you as the authority in your field and catapults your marketing strategy to new heights requires more than just a fleeting aspiration. It necessitates a meticulously crafted blueprint.

This blueprint is your roadmap, guiding every step from conception to publication, ensuring your book not only reaches completion but achieves its purpose – transforming your expertise into a powerful marketing tool that generates a flood of pre-qualified leads.

This chapter provides a brief overview of our plan before we dive deeper into it in the following chapters.

Setting your intentions

Begin by setting clear, achievable goals for your book. What do you wish to accomplish? Whether it's establishing credibility in your industry, generating leads or providing value that converts readers into loyal customers, your goals will steer the book's direction. Be specific. A goal to 'grow my business' is commendable, but a goal to 'increase lead generation by 20 percent through educational content' gives you a target and a way to measure success.

Understanding your audience

No message, no matter how expertly crafted, will have an impact if it doesn't resonate with its intended audience. Therefore, your second step is to gain a deep understanding of who you are writing for.

Who are your ideal clients or customers? What challenges do they face that you have the expertise to solve? This understanding will not only inform the content of your book, but also how you approach its tone, structure and promotional strategies.

Conduct surveys, analyse feedback from your current clients, and engage with your target audience on social media to gather insights into their needs and preferences. This research will highlight the pain points and aspirations of your audience, providing a solid foundation for your book's content. Refer back to Chapter 8 if you need to.

Crafting your unique value proposition

With your audience in mind, consider what unique perspective or solution you can offer. Your book should not be a reiteration of common knowledge, but should provide fresh insights, innovative strategies or unique stories that only you can tell.

This unique value proposition (UVP) will set your book apart from the myriad of resources already available to your audience. It's what makes your book not just another item on the shelf but a must-read. Refer back to Chapter 7 if you are yet to find a unique angle for your book.

Establishing a writing schedule

The final step in planning your authority book is to create a writing schedule. Writing a book in 28 days is an ambitious goal, requiring discipline and time management. Break down your writing process into daily or weekly word count targets, taking into account your current commitments and working style.

Some authors find it helpful to dedicate specific blocks of time each day to writing, while others may prefer intensive writing sessions a few times a week. Find what works best for you and stick to it. Consistency is key. Break it down and work backwards. For example, if you want your book to have around 100,000 words, and be written within 28 days, you would need to write approximately 3,571 words a day if you write every day without fail. This is a challenging but achievable goal.

Outlining your book

With your goals set, audience defined and UVP clarified, it's time to outline your book. This outline will serve as a skeleton for your manuscript, organising your thoughts and ensuring a logical flow of information. Each chapter should build on the last, guiding your reader through a journey that not only educates but also engages.

Start with broad strokes, outlining the major sections or parts of your book, then break these down into individual chapters. For each chapter, list the key points or messages you want to convey. This process not only makes writing more manageable by breaking the book into smaller sections, but also ensures that each chapter aligns with your overall objectives. The next chapter will dive deeper into this process.

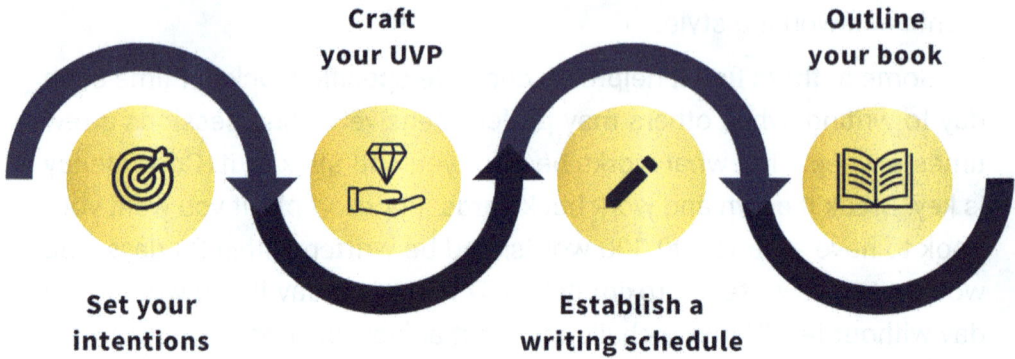

Figure 9: Laying the foundations of your book

The journey to writing a book that elevates your authority and amplifies your marketing efforts begins with a solid plan. By setting clear goals, understanding your audience, defining your unique value proposition, outlining your book, and establishing a disciplined writing schedule, you are laying the foundation for success.

"

'If you fail to plan, you are planning to fail.'

BENJAMIN FRANKLIN

POLYMATH, WRITER, SCIENTIST, INVENTOR, STATESMAN, DIPLOMAT, PRINTER, PUBLISHER AND POLITICAL PHILOSOPHER (AKA A VERY WISE DUDE)

Define your goals

Objective: To take the time to understand what you want to achieve by writing this book.

1. What specific outcomes do you want to achieve with your book? (e.g. establish credibility, increase lead generation by 20 percent, sell x number of books per day, which means x% of high-ticket calls booked resulting in x sales).
2. How will you measure the success of these goals?
3. How do you want to feel when you finally publish your book?
4. How will you celebrate your achievements?

You can do this exercise on a piece of paper, or if you'd like to download a digital version of this worksheet, scan the QR code below:

CHAPTER 13

STRUCTURING YOUR BOOK
Crafting a Compelling Narrative

If you're writing a non-fiction book (and I assume you are because you're reading this book), then the structure of your manuscript is critical. It will be the framework on which your ideas, insights and stories are built. It's what transforms a collection of thoughts into a coherent, impactful narrative that guides your readers through a journey – from identifying their initial problem to understanding and implementing your solutions.

Your book must be well organised and easy to read if you want it to be successful. In this chapter, we will lay down that framework, ensuring your book is not just informative but also engaging and transformative.

Understanding the importance of structure

A well-structured book facilitates learning, retention and application. It makes complex information accessible and actionable. For your readers, the structure of your book is a roadmap highlighting the path from where they are now to where they want to be after reading it.

For you, it's a blueprint that organises your thoughts and ensures your message is conveyed clearly and effectively. Without this blueprint, it is easy to get overwhelmed and end up doing nothing.

Defining your core message

First things first – the cornerstone of your book is the overarching theme or core message. Before diving into chapter outlines, it's crucial to define the core message. It's like the North Star guiding you through the vast expanse of your narrative universe.

Take a moment to reflect on what your book is all about. What is the single, most important takeaway you want your readers to have? This core message should be the golden thread that runs through your book, ensuring each section and chapter contributes to and reinforces this central theme. Refer back to Chapter 7 if needed.

Once you've got this central theme firmly in your grasp, it's time to roll up your sleeves and start the magic. Picture your book as a puzzle with the chapters as pieces that form the bigger picture. Each chapter is like a miniature adventure, a journey within the grand expedition of your main idea.

Let's say your book is a guide to parenting girls aged three to seven. (Fantastic choice!) Now, imagine your theme as the heartbeat of your parenting journey or your unique method. In the chapters, you get to explore and dissect different facets of that journey, like a skilled surgeon operating on your story.

For instance, one chapter could be all about discipline – the art of balance between setting boundaries and fostering independence – a roadmap for parents navigating the sometimes turbulent waters of raising small humans.

Then there's the chapter on communication, where you delve into the intricate dance of words between parents and their little ones. It's not just about talking, it's about creating a language of understanding and connection, essential steps in the parenting waltz.

And let's not forget the chapter on activities for children – the treasure trove of ideas to spark creativity, curiosity and maybe a bit of controlled chaos. From arts and crafts to outdoor adventures, this chapter is perhaps the playground of your parenting manual.

See, each chapter is like a subplot, a unique facet of your theme that adds depth and richness to your overall narrative. It's the difference between reading a book and embarking on a literary expedition, where every chapter is a new territory waiting to be explored.

Creating a chapter outline

With your core message in hand, begin outlining your chapters. Start with the broad sections or parts of your book, each representing a key stage in the reader's journey. Within each section, list the chapters, and for each chapter, outline the main points or arguments you plan to cover.

This approach breaks the writing process into manageable pieces and ensures that each chapter aligns with the overall structure and flow of the book. All while flipping the middle finger to overwhelm. Magical, right?

The building begins

Once you have a basic outline of your chapters, you can start to flesh out each one with more detailed information. As you write, keep in mind that every chapter should flow smoothly from one topic to the next. You don't want your readers to feel like they're reading a textbook, so make sure your writing is engaging and easy to follow.

A typical non-fiction book will include the following:

- ✓ Dedication (optional)
- ✓ Introduction
- ✓ Chapters (which may be sectioned off into parts)
- ✓ Conclusion

✓ Acknowledgements (optional)
✓ About the Author (optional)
✓ Helpful resources (optional)

1. A dedication

The inclusion of a dedication at the beginning of a book is a poignant and heartfelt tradition that allows you to express gratitude, love or appreciation to individuals who have played significant roles in your life or in the creation of the book itself. Whether dedicated to family members, friends, mentors or sources of inspiration, these words convey a sense of connection, adding depth to the reader's experience and creating an intimate link between you and your audience.

In essence, a dedication is a sincere acknowledgement that goes beyond the narrative, fostering a sense of shared humanity and connection through the written word. Note that this is different to the acknowledgement section. Check out some of your favourite books for inspiration.

2. Lay the foundation: the introduction

Every building needs a solid foundation, and your book is no different. Your introduction is the bedrock that sets the tone for the entire journey through your building. It's the hook that reels readers in and the teaser that promises excitement. Make it engaging, make it compelling and, most importantly, make it crystal clear what your book is all about.

Remember, this is where you establish your author voice, your unique style. Don't be afraid to infuse some personality into it. You're inviting readers into your world, so make it a welcoming entrance.

3. The pillars: main sections or parts

Now that you've hooked your readers, let's talk about the main sections or parts of your book. Think of these as the pillars that support the structure. Each part should have a clear purpose and take your readers on a logical journey. It's like walking through a well-organised museum where each section has its own theme, but taken together they tell a complete and cohesive story.

Divide your content strategically. If your book is a how-to guide, maybe each part corresponds to a different phase of the process. If it's a historical exploration, perhaps each part covers a distinct era. Whatever your subject, ensure that each part serves a purpose in advancing your narrative.

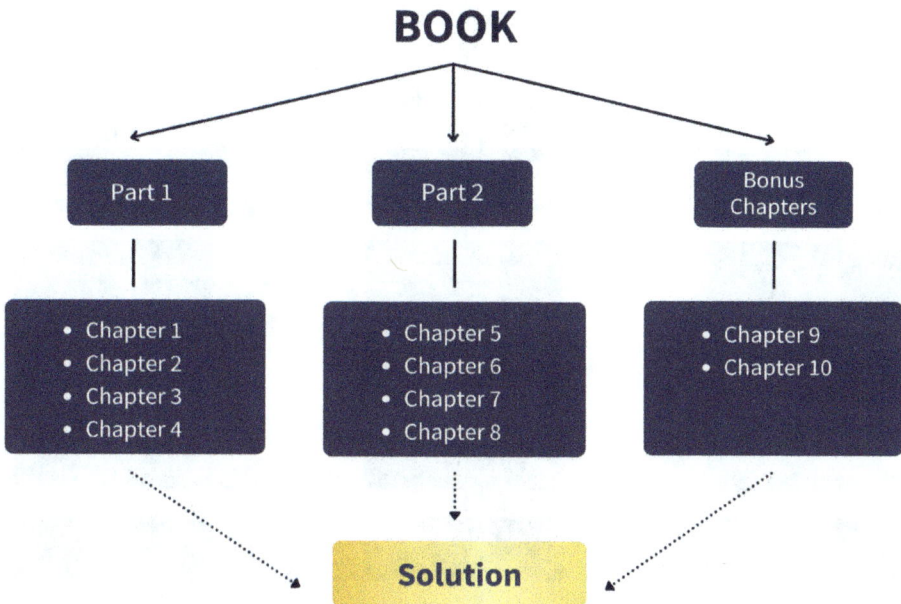

BOOK

Part 1	Part 2	Bonus Chapters
• Chapter 1 • Chapter 2 • Chapter 3 • Chapter 4	• Chapter 5 • Chapter 6 • Chapter 7 • Chapter 8	• Chapter 9 • Chapter 10

Solution

Figure 10: How your book blueprint begins

4. The framework: chapters within parts

Within each part, you have the chapters – your framework. These are the rooms in your building. See it as giving a guided tour as you lead visitors from one room to the next, starting on the ground floor and working your way up through the house, ensure your chapters flow logically. One idea should lead to the next, creating a smooth transition for your readers.

Feel free to get creative with your chapter titles. They're like labels, guiding your readers through the layout of your narrative. Make the titles intriguing, make them irresistible, and make sure they accurately reflect the content within.

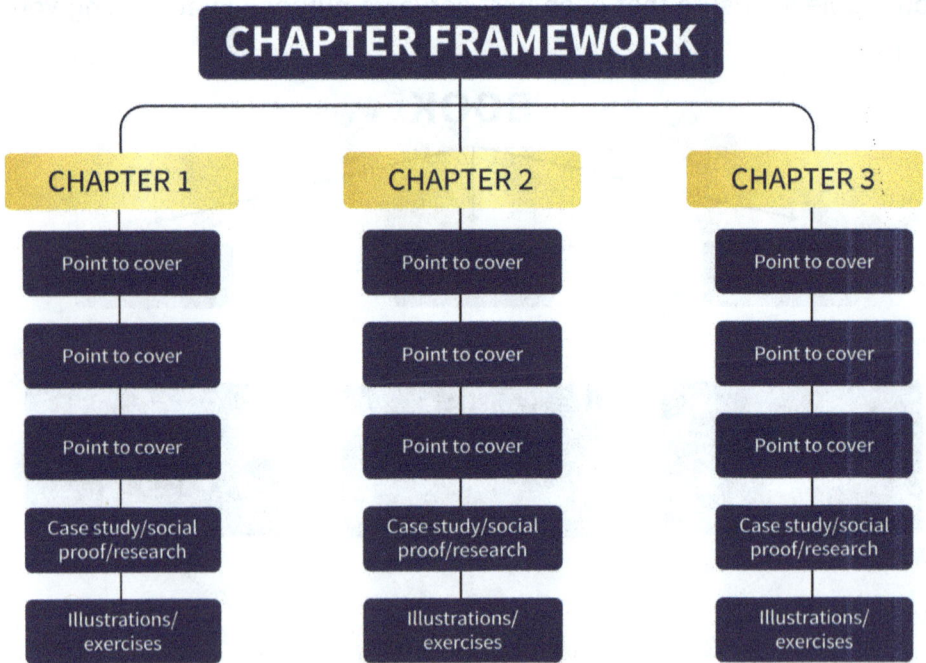

CHAPTER FRAMEWORK

CHAPTER 1	CHAPTER 2	CHAPTER 3
Point to cover	Point to cover	Point to cover
Point to cover	Point to cover	Point to cover
Point to cover	Point to cover	Point to cover
Case study/social proof/research	Case study/social proof/research	Case study/social proof/research
Illustrations/ exercises	Illustrations/ exercises	Illustrations/ exercises

Figure 11: Chapter framework showing how you would go about planning what to include in each chapter

5. Windows and doors: subheadings and transitions

As we move through the building (chapter), let's talk about subheadings and transitions. Subheadings act like windows, offering glimpses into what's to come. They break up the text, providing breathing space for your readers. Transitions, on the other hand, are the doors that smoothly usher readers from one idea to the next. A continuous flow with no abrupt stops.

Ensure your subheadings are clear and concise, offering a plan for what lies ahead. Transitions should be seamless, like walking from one room to another without tripping over the threshold.

6. The rooftop: conclusion

Finally, we reach the rooftop – the conclusion. This is where you offer panoramic views of the insights gained, tying everything together. Don't leave your readers stranded on the roof. Guide them gently back to solid ground. Revisit the key points, leave them with a memorable takeaway and bid them farewell with a sense of fulfilment.

And don't forget to once again invite your readers to take action and join you outside the pages of your book and inside your business.

6A. Sales opportunity

You could include another section of the book in between the conclusion and the acknowledgements designed to make a direct invitation to the reader to come and work with you. You could invite them to join your free group, receive a complimentary strategy call, download a bonus additional resource, and so on. If you don't ask, you don't get.

As long as you focus on what the reader will gain rather than what you are offering, you will experience success.

7. Acknowledgements

Including acknowledgements at the end of a book is a thoughtful practice that allows authors to thank the people who played a significant role in the creation and realisation of their work.

These acknowledgements often extend beyond the author's immediate circle to encompass editors, publishers, family members, friends and mentors who have offered support, guidance and inspiration throughout the writing process.

It serves as a genuine gesture of appreciation, recognising the collaborative nature of the creative journey and acknowledging the contributions of those who may have otherwise remained behind the scenes. This section adds another personal touch to the book.

8. About the author

Including an 'About the Author' section at the end of a book provides another glimpse into the person behind the words, in this case, you. It serves as a personal connection, offering insights into your background, experiences and motivations that you may not have been able to communicate earlier in the book. This section often highlights your expertise, achievements and other works, fostering a sense of trust and familiarity between you and the reader. It's basically your professional biography. Don't forget to include your contact details and social links in this part.

9. Helpful resources

Including a section like this is a valuable extension of your commitment to providing comprehensive and practical assistance to your readers. This section typically compiles a curated list of references, further reading material, online sources and tools related to the book's subject matter. This can include links to your own resources as well as those of others you know your reader will value on their journey.

These are your basic building blocks, but there is some other stuff you need to consider ...

Balancing theory and practice

A compelling book offers a mix of theory (to educate) and practice (to empower). While it's essential to ground your readers in the concepts and strategies you're sharing, it's equally important to show them how to apply these in real life. Include case studies, exercises, templates or action steps in your chapters. This balance makes your book engaging and valuable, providing readers with the tools they need to enact real change.

Don't be scared to give it all away. People will read your book and buy your stuff even if you just gave them everything they need within the pages. Most people need more incentive to get off their butts and really do something.

Incorporating stories and examples

Stories and examples breathe life into your book. They illustrate your points in a way that facts and figures alone cannot. Share stories from your own experience, your clients' successes and failures or well-known examples from your industry.

These narratives should serve to reinforce your core message, making the abstract tangible and the complex understandable.

Planning for engagement

Consider how you will engage readers throughout the book. This might include prompts for reflection, questions to ponder, checklists or challenges. Engagement techniques like these make your book interactive, encouraging readers not just to consume information passively but actively engage with it, deepening their understanding and retention.

The role of introductions and conclusions

Each chapter should have a clear introduction that outlines what the reader can expect to learn and a conclusion that summarises key takeaways and next steps. This structure makes your book easy to follow while reinforcing learning for your readers, ensuring they come away with a clear understanding of how to apply what they've read to their own lives and businesses.

Structuring your book is both an art and a science. It requires a careful balance of theory and practice, a strategic use of stories and examples, and a constant focus on engaging and guiding your readers.

By crafting a compelling narrative structure, you ensure your book is not just read but remembered and acted upon, solidifying your status as an authority in your field and making your book an invaluable asset to your marketing strategy.

To help with implementing this chapter, I created an additional book bonus called The Manuscript Mapping System Blueprint, which will help you organise your ideas and structure your book effectively, ensuring a coherent and compelling story. You can access this bonus by scanning the QR code below:

"

Without a clear structure to base your writing on, you will likely fall into the abyss of overwhelm and become bedfellows with procrastination. This will not get your book written. Create a structure and then follow it to the end. One word in front of the other is how we get to where we want to go.

TARRYN REEVES

AUTHOR, PUBLISHER AND SPEAKER

The structure of your book

Objective: To map out the structure of your book so you have a solid blueprint to follow until the final page.

Section 1: Defining Your Core Message

1. **Identify your core message:** What is the single, most important takeaway you want your readers to have? Write a concise statement of your book's core message.

2. **Reflect on the core message:** How does this message guide the structure of your book? How will each chapter contribute to this central theme?

Section 2: Planning Your Book's Structure

1. **List main sections/parts:** What are the broad sections or parts of your book? Each part should represent a key stage in the reader's journey. Write down the titles of these sections along with a brief description of their purpose.

2. **Outline chapters:** For each section listed above, outline the chapters it will contain. Include a title and a brief summary of the main points or arguments of each chapter. They don't have to be your final choice but will act as a starting point.

3. **Details for each chapter:** Choose one chapter to start with and answer the following questions to add more detail:

   - What are the main points and arguments covered in this chapter?
   - How does this chapter contribute to the book's core message?

- What stories or examples will you include to illustrate your points?
- What practical advice, exercises or action steps will you provide?

Section 3: Fleshing Out Your Book

1. **Engagement strategies:** How will you engage readers throughout the book? List any prompts for reflection, questions, checklists or challenges you plan to include.
2. **Balancing theory and practice:** How will you balance educational content with actionable advice? Provide examples of how you will incorporate both these aspects into your book.
3. **Using stories and examples:** List the stories and examples you plan to use to illustrate your points. Indicate in which chapter each will be included and how the story/example reinforces your core message.

Section 4: The Building Blocks of Your Book

1. **Introduction:** Draft a brief outline of your introduction. How will you hook your readers and set the tone for the book?
2. **Conclusion:** Outline your conclusion. How will you tie everything together and leave your readers with a memorable takeaway?
3. **Dedication and acknowledgements:** Think about who you want to dedicate your book to and who you want to acknowledge. List these individuals and briefly note why.
4. **About the author:** Draft a brief biography highlighting your expertise, achievements and any other works. Don't forget to include something personal – readers warm to having something in common with you.

5. **Helpful resources:** Compile a list of helpful resources, references and tools you plan to include in your book. Indicate whether they relate to specific chapters or the book as a whole.

Section 5: Review and Refinement

1. **Review your worksheet:** Go through each section of your worksheet. Are there any areas that need more detail or clarification?
2. **Feedback:** Consider sharing your worksheet with a trusted peer or mentor for feedback. Are there any suggestions to improve your book's structure?

Things to Remember

- Remember, structuring your book is an iterative process. Be open to revising your outline as your ideas evolve.
- Keep your core message at the forefront of your planning. Every chapter, every section should contribute to this central theme.
- Consider your reader's journey from start to finish. Your book should guide the reader through a transformation, offering a clear path from problem to solution.

You can do this exercise on a piece of paper, or if you'd like to download a digital version of this worksheet, scan the QR code below:

Non-Fiction Chapter Structure Worksheet

Objective: To help you structure each chapter.

Please note that you should use this template only as you see fit. You don't want to sound like a robot, so if your intuition is telling you to leave something out or that something doesn't quite work for a particular chapter, then leave it out!

Outline your chapters

- **Chapter sequence:** Number your chapters.
- **Chapter title:** Give your chapters a name.
- **Objective:** What is the goal of this chapter? What do you want the reader to learn or understand by the end of it?
- **Key points:** List the main points you want to cover in this chapter. These can be subtopics, arguments or questions that will guide the content.

    1.

    2.

    3.

    4.

- **Introduction:** A brief paragraph introducing the chapter's main ideas and what the reader can expect to learn.

- **Content sections:** Break the chapter into sections based on the key points listed. For each section, provide a brief description or bullet points of what will be covered.

    Section 1: Description or bullet points.

    Section 2: Description or bullet points.

- **Case Studies or examples:** Include any real-life examples, case studies, or anecdotes that will help illustrate your points. Describe them briefly and explain how they relate to the chapter's content.

- **Sidebars/boxes (optional):** If you plan to include sidebars or information boxes, describe what they will contain. This can be additional information, tips, quotes or statistics related to the content.

- **Conclusion:** Summarise the key points in the chapter and reiterate how they support the chapter's objective. You might also want to link to the theme of the next chapter to provide a smooth transition.

- **Call to action (optional):** If relevant, end the chapter with a call to action, encouraging the reader to apply what they've learned, reflect on a specific question or proceed to the next chapter with a particular thought in mind.

- **References/further reading:** List any references and sources, or suggest further reading materials that support your chapter's content.

Additional notes

- **Illustrations/graphics needed:** List any illustrations, charts, graphs or other graphics that will enhance the chapter's content.

- **Research notes:** Include any specific research findings, statistics or data that need to be cited or incorporated into the chapter.

- **Interviews/expert contributions:** List any interviews or expert contributions that will be included in the chapter, along with the topics they will address.

You can do this exercise on a piece of paper, or if you'd like to download a digital version of this worksheet, scan the QR code below:

SECTION 3

WRITING YOUR BOOK

CHAPTER 14

THE WRITER'S TOOLBOX

There is no one way to write to get the words out of your head and heart and on to paper. The idea that many of us have of an author is of a person sitting in their romantic writing space all day, easily putting pen to paper or fingers to keyboard, undisturbed and in the creative flow.

The reality is that few of us can operate this way and we certainly need to find a way to fit our writing into all the other parts of our lives that we juggle daily.

This chapter is dedicated to the magical realm of writing tools and techniques. Just as a carpenter relies on a trusty hammer, and a chef cherishes a well-worn knife, writers also have an arsenal of instruments at their disposal. There are different techniques and tools that can make the process easier. In this chapter, I share some of my favourites.

Create a writing routine

One way to make writing easier is to have a set routine or process that you follow each time you sit down to write. This might involve setting up your workspace in a certain way, lighting a candle, making a cup of tea or playing some calming music. It might also involve setting a timer for a certain period and agreeing with yourself that during that time you will not allow anything else to distract you.

Once you have established this routine it will become easier and quicker to settle into the writing zone each time you sit at your desk.

Going old school

In an age dominated by keyboards and touchscreens, the classic pen and paper still hold a special place in many writers' hearts. There's something about the tactile connection between hand and page that can unleash a torrent of inspiration. Whether it's a leather-bound journal or a napkin grabbed in a coffee shop, the simplicity of this duo is a timeless ally for capturing thoughts on the fly.

Outline your chapters

This one is for the stationary lovers out there!

Grab yourself a pack of those handy study cards or even a pack of sticky notes.

Write your chapter titles at the top of each card, one chapter per card. Below the title, jot down a few key concepts you want to cover in that chapter.

As you finish the cards, stick or pin them in order on a wall, or lay them on a table or the floor. This gives you a bird's-eye view of all your ideas. Tweak them as needed, move cards around and keep at it until you're 100 percent satisfied with your overall book outline.

Now, the tricky part – resist the urge to dive into writing a chapter before you finish all your cards. It might feel like you're being productive but it's really a sneaky form of procrastination. Trust me, your brain will come up with all sorts of reasons to avoid the hard work of outlining!

These cards will be your trusty guide when you start writing your book, so make sure you scribble enough notes on each card to write for at least 10 minutes on the topic. Don't go cramming heaps of content into one chapter. Keep it short and sweet. Stick to high-value ideas and get that book done.

Writing prompts

Another useful tool is what I like to call the 'writing prompt'. This can be anything from a question you need to answer to a picture or word that you need to write about. Having a prompt to focus on can help prevent the dreaded writer's block and kick-start your writing.

Free writing

If you find yourself getting stuck, or if your mind starts to wander, another helpful technique is what is known as 'free writing'. This involves setting a timer for a certain amount of time (usually between five and 10 minutes) and then simply writing down whatever comes into your head without stopping or editing yourself.

The aim is not to produce something perfect but simply to get the words forming and to allow your creative juices to start flowing. Once the timer goes off you can then go back and edit what you have written if you wish.

The digital scribe

For those who've embraced the digital age, a keyboard is the weapon of choice. From sleek laptops to clickety-clack mechanical keyboards, the act of typing can be a dance of fingers translating thoughts into pixels. Word processing programs like Microsoft Word, Google Docs, Grammarly, Hemingway Editor or Scrivener have become the modern-day parchment, offering a slew of features to organise, edit and polish your prose.

Mind mapping

Enter the realm of mind maps where chaos meets creativity. Tools like MindMeister or a good old-fashioned whiteboard can help you visualise connections between ideas. Unleash your inner cartographer and watch your thoughts sprawl across the page like uncharted territories waiting to be explored.

Read-aloud ritual

Ever tried reading your work aloud? The ears, it turns out, can be as discerning as the eyes. Hearing your sentences dance in the air can reveal awkward phrasing, stumbling rhythms and the occasional tongue-twisting typo. So, find a quiet space, channel your inner Shakespeare and let the words echo.

I've also found it useful to have someone else read my words back to me. That way I can hear how a reader who is unfamiliar with the book is experiencing the sentence flow.

ChatGPT

It would be remiss of me not to include a short piece on the use of ChatGPT for writing a book. Using ChatGPT can be a valuable and efficient tool to enhance your creative process. Please note the use of the word enhance here. I do not believe that ChatGPT can write a good quality book nor do I believe it can compensate for a lack of knowledge or creativity on your part.

What the ChatGPT tool can do is help you to overcome creative blocks, generate ideas and get inspiration. It can also be a brainstorming partner, offering diverse perspectives and imaginative input that you may not otherwise have considered. It can also be a helpful resource for researching and fact-checking.

Simply put, ChatGPT works best when it complements your creativity. You must do the work and ensure that your own words hold the essence of your unique voice and vision for your book.

Remember that these are but tools – extensions of your writing. Experiment, mix and match, and forge your own path. The art of writing is a deeply personal journey. The tools you choose are the companions that walk beside you on this literary adventure.

"

'Work hard but work smart.
Always. Every day.'

BOBBI BROWN

MAKE-UP ARTIST, AUTHOR AND FOUNDER OF
BOBBI BROWN COSMETICS

CHAPTER 15

MORE THAN ONE WAY TO WRITE

If you've been stressing out that you have to write your book the 'normal' way, then I have good news. There is no wrong way to write your book. Gone are the days where the writer had to sit down with typewriter or pen and paper, or even fingers over a keyboard if that's not your jam. Nope. You have other options and you get to do this in whichever way works best for you.

I like to group my writers into three loose styles. You may flit between styles but there will definitely be one that fits you best.

The traditional writer

First up, we have the traditional writer. This is the lone warrior, armed with nothing but a blank page and the uncanny ability to weave words effortlessly. If you find yourself nodding along, then congrats, my friend, you might just be a traditionalist.

You're the kind of person who can sit down and let the words flow from your mind to the page like a well-practised dance (except during those bouts of writer's block from which we all suffer). No overthinking, no second-guessing – just pure, unadulterated writing magic.

The talkative writer

Then there's the talkative writer, the wordsmith who finds their muse in the sound of their own voice. If you're the type who thinks best when speaking aloud, this might be your writing home. Grab your phone, hit record and let your thoughts spill out like a literary confessional. Later, transcribe your vocal symphony into a more structured format.

And hey, if you're feeling tech-savvy, let 'voice to text' features in programs like Google Docs do the heavy lifting. Who knew talking to yourself could be so productive?

The buddy up writer

Last but not least, we've got the buddy up writer – the social butterfly of the writing world. If you find your creativity sparked by conversation, then this style might be your sweet spot. Imagine setting up a cosy meeting with a friend and letting the ideas bounce back and forth like a game of intellectual tennis. Record the banter, get it transcribed and 'voila' – you've got the raw material for your masterpiece.

And even consider getting yourself a writing buddy for the long haul – someone to share the highs, lows and countless plot twists with as you navigate the tumultuous seas of creativity.

So, which camp do you fall into? Are you a lone wolf facing the blank page, a vocal virtuoso serenading your ideas, or a social scribe thriving on collaborative energy? Whatever your style, embrace it. After all, the writing world is your oyster, and you've got the pen in hand – or voice recorder – to craft your own narrative masterpiece. Happy writing!

"

'It's important to remember that there is no right way to write. The most important thing is to find a process and set of tools that work for you and that help you to get the words down on paper in a way that feels comfortable for you.'

TARRYN REEVES

AUTHOR, PUBLISHER AND SPEAKER

CHAPTER 16

GATHERING CONTENT FOR YOUR BOOK

It can be tough to know where to find information and how to organise it all. In this chapter, I'll give you some tips on easy ways to gather content for your non-fiction book. I am a big fan of working smarter and not harder. I'm sure you are, too.

Writing a non-fiction book really comes down to answering questions.

Some questions relating to your chosen topic to ask yourself and then find answers for are:

- Who?
- What?
- Where?
- When?
- Why?
- How?
- FAQs

You probably have a lot of this information scattered about the place already, so this is more of a hunting and gathering exercise, modern entrepreneur style.

Harness the power of Google

Alrighty! We're really gearing up to pen that non-fiction masterpiece now, which means you're going to need some serious research muscle. Lucky for you, you're writing in the age of Google, so let's dive into how you can harness Google's power to uncover the gems that will make your non-fiction book shine.

1. Nail down your mission

Before you plunge into the vast internet ocean, set your compass straight. What are you hunting for? Define your research goals, mark your territories and chart a course. Outline the key themes, topics and questions you need to explore. This will help you stay on track, focused and efficient during your research time.

2. Go ninja with advanced search tricks

Want in on some Google secret sauce? It's called advanced search operators, and it's like having a ninja guide to help you find exactly what you need. Google loves it when you speak its language.

Some operators include:

- Quotation marks (" or '): Use quotes to search for an exact phrase. For example, 'climate change effects' will return results with that specific phrase.
- Site: Limit your search to a specific website or domain. For instance, site: wikipedia.org 'renewable energy' will provide results only from Wikipedia.
- Filetype: Narrow your search to specific file types, such as PDF or PPT. For example, 'sustainable agriculture' filetype:pdf will yield PDF documents on sustainable agriculture.

3. Academic adventures with Google Scholar

Feeling a bit scholarly? Google Scholar is your ivory tower. Dive into the world of academic articles, theses and the brainy stuff (nerds like me love this). Drop some serious keywords to open the doors to a treasure trove of scholarly wisdom. But remember to take this information and use it in your book in a way that speaks to the everyday person. There's nothing worse than reading a book that feels like a textbook from university days.

4. Keep your ear to the ground with Google Alerts

Want to stay ahead of the game? Set up Google Alerts as your trusty news hound. It barks when there's fresh info on the block. Set it up for your keywords, and let it fetch the latest updates straight to your inbox. It's the entrepreneurial writer's best friend.

5. Bookworm's delight: Google Books

For the bookish vibes, Google Books is your sanctuary. Preview, snack on and devour digitised books, magazines and articles. It's like a buffet for bookworms, with citations and references sprinkled in for extra flavour.

6. Surf the trends with Google Trends

If your book's about catching the zeitgeist, (meaning the latest trend. I just like that word. It sounds fancy and, well, I'm a major word nerd. Check out my Insta stories, which are usually full of random words and their meanings. Sorry … not sorry.) then Google Trends is your crystal ball. See what the internet's buzzing about and ride the wave of trends. It's like a sneak peek into what people are curious about right now.

7. Fact-check 101

As Sherlock would say (what a legend!) 'Double-checking the facts would be elementary.' Cross-reference like your book's reputation depends on it. Because it does. Check author credentials and publication dates, and make sure your sources aren't spinning yarns.

8. Organise like a boss

As you gather the treasure trove of information you will use to craft your book, keep it tidy. Use Google Drive, note-taking apps – whatever floats your research boat. Organise your findings so that when the writing storm hits, you're ready to set sail with a well-provisioned boat.

Please don't give me hives and have your research look like an organisational bomb has exploded. You'll thank me later – promise.

So, there you have it, your guide to using Google like a boss for your non-fiction masterpiece. With ninja-like search skills, scholarly prowess and a finger on the trending pulse, you're armed and ready. But – wait... there's more!

Unlock the power of expert interviews

Another great way to gather content for your book is to interview experts in your field. This can provide first-hand accounts and valuable information that you can use in your book. Let's talk about why interviewing experts could be a game-changer for your writing.

1. Authenticity beyond words

Imagine having access to real-life stories straight from the horse's mouth. When you interview experts, you're not just collecting data, you're capturing the essence of their experiences. Whether it's a successful entrepreneur, a seasoned scientist or a renowned artist, these individuals bring a level of authenticity that you can't achieve through research alone.

Think about it – readers love stories that resonate with real life. Anecdotes, triumphs and failures – these are all ingredients that will make your book relatable and memorable. Expert interviews provide the authenticity that can turn a good book into a remarkable one.

2. Insider knowledge unveiled

Experts haven't become experts by accident. They've dedicated years to mastering their craft and accumulating knowledge that can't be found in textbooks. By sitting down with these authorities, you gain access to insider information that might not be readily available to the public.

This insider knowledge not only enriches your content but also positions your book as a go-to resource for readers seeking a deeper understanding of the subject. It's like offering your audience a backstage pass to the inner workings of your field, and who wouldn't want that?

3. Building credibility and authority

When you cite the insights of experts in your book, you're not just adding substance – you're also borrowing their credibility. Readers are more likely to trust and respect your work when they see that you've consulted experts in the field. It's a subtle way of saying, 'Hey, I've done my homework, and these experts back me up.'

This borrowed credibility goes a long way in establishing your authority as an author. Having the experts' endorsement can make your book stand out in a crowded market.

4. Networking opportunities

Interviewing experts isn't just about what they can offer your book, it's also about building relationships. As you connect with these professionals, you open doors to potential collaborations, endorsements and future projects. Networking with experts in your field can extend the lifespan of your book beyond its pages.

That expert you interview today might be the key to a future book launch event, a podcast interview or even a joint venture. The relationships you cultivate during the interview process can turn into long-lasting connections that benefit your current project and your future endeavours.

5. The human element

Books are not just repositories of information. They're also windows into the human experience. Expert interviews bring a human touch to your writing. It's not just about facts and figures, it's about the people behind them. This human element adds depth and emotion to your book, making it more engaging and relatable.

Interviewing these experts is easier than you think. Many experts are more than willing to share their knowledge, especially if they see the value in your work. They may even write a foreword for your book.

I haven't mentioned a foreword before now because they aren't necessary. A foreword is a short introduction to a book written by someone else (not the author). I suggest that if you choose to have a foreword that it be written by an expert in a similar field.

Unleash the power of surveys and polls

Another way to gather content is to conduct surveys or polls. This can be a great way to get feedback from your target audience and see what information they are looking for, thus allowing you to tailor your content to their exact desires.

You've now done your ideal reader research and know exactly who it is you are writing for, but rather than assuming, why not just ask what it is they want? To create a killer survey, keep it simple, engaging and, most importantly, relevant.

If you're writing a self-help book, for example, inquire about the challenges people face and the solutions they're seeking. (This could also help you craft your next-level offer, which you may wish to sell off the back end of your book. This is, after all, lead-generation magic!)

Don't shy away from multiple-choice questions – they're like little nuggets of shiny gold. They provide structured data that's easy to analyse. Remember, keep it short. Nobody wants to feel like they're taking a final exam.

Use social media, your email list or even your website to spread the word. Offer a little incentive to complete your survey – people love freebies.

Once the data starts rolling in, look for patterns, common themes and unexpected insights. This is where the magic happens – you're not just gathering information. You're discovering the heartbeat of your audience.

You've already done the work

Chances are, you've done a lot of the work for your book already. All the content you have created to date (course content, social posts, podcast interviews, blogs, etc.) is a treasure trove sitting right under your nose. Work smarter not harder and repurpose that gold!

Think about it this way: those newsletters that your subscribers loved, the eBooks that garnered attention, and the insights shared in podcast interviews are like puzzle pieces waiting to come together to form a cohesive narrative. It's not just recycling content – it's giving it a second life, a chance to be part of something bigger.

Remember that gem of an idea you shared in that podcast interview a few months ago? Well, it could be the cornerstone of a chapter in your book. By reviewing your existing content, you're not just saving time, you're also ensuring that the essence of what you've already put out there is preserved and amplified.

And let's not forget the power of consistency. Your audience has come to appreciate your style and voice through your various content channels. Repurposing that content into a book means maintaining that consistency and creating a seamless reading experience for your dedicated followers.

It's not about reinventing the wheel. It's about taking the wheels you've already got and building a better vehicle that can take your audience on a more rewarding journey. Plus, repurposing content is a smart move for efficiency (one of my most favourite things in the world). Why start from scratch when you can build on the foundation you've already laid?

So, dig into those old newsletters, revisit those eBooks, scroll through those social media gems and relive those podcast moments. You might just find the missing pieces to a puzzle you didn't even know you were solving – your own book. It's like mining in your content archives. Trust me, the nuggets you'll uncover will turn out to be pure literary gold.

"

So often people are working hard at the wrong thing. Working on the right thing is probably more important than working hard.

CATERINA FAKE

ENTREPRENEUR AND BUSINESSWOMAN

The Content Gathering Worksheet

Objective: To work smarter and not harder by looking back on work you have already done and could use in your book.

1. What information did you find when searching Google for content related to your topic? Include links so you can go back and reference them later.

2. Are there any experts in your field who you could interview to gather content for your book? Note them and their contact details so you can reach out and schedule a chat.

3. A great way to gather information is to survey your target reader. Note down some questions you could ask when you are ready to send out your survey.

4. Go through content that you have created in the past and take note along with relevant links. Think blogs, podcasts, presentations, social media posts, live videos, etc.

You can do this exercise on a piece of paper, or if you'd like to download a digital version of this worksheet, scan the QR code below:

CHAPTER 17

CONTENT CREATION
Techniques for Clear, Persuasive Writing

Content is the soul of your book. It's what readers will come for and stay for, provided it resonates, educates and motivates them. This chapter focuses on the art and science behind creating content that not only informs but also engages and persuades your audience.

Here, we delve into techniques that elevate your writing from mere word vomit on a page to a compelling narrative that ensures your expertise shines from every line.

Start with a strong hook

The opening of your book, and indeed each chapter, should grab your reader's attention and hold it tight. Begin with a provocative question, a surprising fact or a compelling story. This hook should resonate with your reader's needs, fears, aspirations or curiosities, encouraging them to delve deeper in search of answers or enlightenment.

Simplify complex concepts

One major goal as an authority in your field is to make complex concepts accessible to your audience. Use analogies, metaphors and simple language to explain difficult ideas. Break down the information into manageable, bite-sized pieces, ensuring readers can easily understand and apply what they learn.

Remember, clarity is key. If readers feel lost, they are likely to disengage – and we definitely don't want that.

Tell stories that resonate

Stories are powerful tools for persuasion and connection. They can illustrate abstract concepts, share successes and failures, and allow people to connect with you and your expertise on a genuine human level.

Integrate personal anecdotes or client case studies that highlight the practical application of your advice. Ensure these stories are relevant and relatable, and serve to help readers see themselves in the narrative and understand the real-world impact of your teachings.

Engage with questions and prompts

Involve your readers in the narrative by posing questions or providing prompts that encourage reflection. This engagement makes your book an interactive experience, rather than a passive one, deepening readers' connection to what they are consuming.

It encourages readers to think critically about how the information applies to their own lives or businesses, enhancing the value they get from your book.

Use data and research to bolster your points

Support your arguments and advice with data, research and citations from reputable sources. This adds credibility to your work and gives readers a broader context for your insights. That being said, avoid overwhelming them with jargon and dense academic language – textbooks are out, and impactful storytelling is in. Present data in a way that's easy to understand and directly relevant to your readers' interests and needs.

Focus on benefits, not just features

When discussing your methods, strategies or solutions, emphasise the benefits they offer to the reader. It's not enough to describe what your approach is, you need to make clear why it matters. How will it solve a problem, save time, increase efficiency or improve quality of life?

Make the benefits tangible and specific so readers can easily see the value in what you're proposing.

Write with conviction and authority

Your tone should exude confidence and expertise but without crossing into arrogance. You're guiding readers through your area of knowledge, so it's important to assert your authority with confidence while allowing your authentic self to shine through.

Use a strong, active voice and avoid hedging your statements with qualifiers like 'might' or 'maybe'. It's also important to be open about areas of debate within your field or where further research is needed – this honesty will only enhance your credibility.

Edit for clarity and persuasiveness

After your initial draft, revisit your content with a critical eye, focusing on improving clarity, flow and persuasiveness. Remove any fluff that doesn't add value, clarify points that may be ambiguous and strengthen arguments that feel weak. This editing process is crucial for refining your message and ensuring it resonates as powerfully as possible with your readers.

Crafting compelling content is a blend of artistry and expertise. By starting with a strong hook, simplifying complex concepts, telling resonant stories, engaging with your readers and writing with conviction, you can craft a narrative that educates, inspires and persuades.

Your book is not just a collection of words. It's a vehicle for change, a tool for growth and a testament to your authority in your field. With these content creation techniques, you're well on your way to achieving all of this.

"

All good writing is persuasive writing; persuading the reader to buy what you're selling, to side with you, to believe the tales you tell.

RAMSEY ISLER

PRODUCT LEADER, AUTHOR AND
STARTUP CO-FOUNDER

CHAPTER 18

FINDING YOUR UNIQUE VOICE
The Foundation of Your Success

In the bustling marketplace of ideas, where every entrepreneur, thought leader and expert is vying for attention, your unique voice is not just a tool, it's your beacon. It distinguishes your message from the cacophony of competitors and resonates with your audience on a personal level.

This chapter is dedicated to uncovering, refining and confidently projecting your unique voice through the pages of your book, setting the stage for unparalleled connection, engagement and influence.

The essence of your unique voice

Your unique voice is the embodiment of your personality, experiences, values and expertise. It's how you express your message in a way that is inherently yours. Unlike the fleeting trends that dominate the digital landscape, your voice is timeless, fostering a deep sense of trust and reliability with your readers.

Finding your voice starts with introspection. Reflect on what drives you, your journey to where you are now and the lessons you've learned along the way. Consider how you communicate your ideas when you feel most passionate and alive. Is your style formal and analytical, or casual and conversational? Do you prefer to inspire with stories, or convince with data? These reflections are the building blocks of your unique voice.

Authenticity as your compass

In the quest to stand out, there's a temptation to adopt a persona you think will appeal to your audience. However, this approach is unsustainable and ultimately counterproductive, not to mention exhausting. Authenticity is magnetic. It draws people to you and keeps them coming back. Your book should be an extension of your most authentic self, offering readers a genuine connection. Some people won't like you and that's OK. It's their loss!

To ensure your voice remains authentic, write as you speak. Imagine explaining your book's concept to a friend or mentor. How would you describe it? What language would you use? This exercise helps strip away any pretence, revealing the heart of your authentic voice. Feels free, doesn't it?

Consistency across the board

Your unique voice should be consistent, not just within the confines of your book but across all your platforms, blog, podcast, social media or public speaking engagements.

I'll never forget the day I first spoke on a stage in Las Vegas. One of the first words was not very ladylike at all. Turns out part of being authentically me is using a few occasional cuss words to express myself.

This consistency strengthens your brand, making your message instantly recognisable, no matter where it's encountered.

To achieve this, create a voice guideline that outlines the key characteristics of your voice – tone, style, language. List examples of how it manifests in your writing. Refer back to this guideline as you write, ensuring each sentence and paragraph resonates with the core of your unique voice.

Cultivating your voice through practice

Finding and honing your voice is a journey that unfolds with practice. The more you write, the more your voice will emerge and evolve. Encourage feedback from trusted peers or mentors who understand your goals and can provide constructive insights into how your voice comes across in your writing.

Experiment with different writing formats and styles. Write blog posts, articles or even social media captions with the intent of expressing your ideas in various ways. Each medium can offer insights and strengthen various facets of your voice.

Overcoming fear of vulnerability

Expressing your unique voice requires vulnerability and a willingness to put your true self out there for the world to see. It's natural to feel apprehensive about being judged or misunderstood. However, it's this very vulnerability that fosters connection and trust with your readers. Embrace it.

Remember, your book is a bridge between your expertise and your audience's needs. Let your authentic voice be the foundation of that bridge.

Your unique voice is your most powerful asset that not only asserts your authority but also deeply engages and resonates with your audience. By investing the time to discover, refine and consistently apply your authentic voice, you lay the groundwork for a book that stands out in a crowded market.

Your voice is the echo of your brand, the signature of your message, and the key to unlocking unprecedented levels of connection and influence.

"

Being different and thinking differently make a person unforgettable. History does not remember the forgettable. It honours the unique minority the majority cannot forget.

SUZY KASSEM

POET

Discovering the essence of your unique voice

Objective: To identify and understand the core elements that make up your unique voice.

Your unique voice is a blend of your personality, experiences, values and expertise. It's timeless and fosters trust with your audience. Discovering your voice involves introspection and reflection on your passions, style and communication preferences.

1. **Reflect on your journey:** Write about your path to where you are now, including key lessons learned

2. **Identify your style:** Describe how you communicate when you feel most passionate. Are you formal or conversational?

3. **Preferences in expression:** Do you prefer storytelling or data-driven arguments? Provide examples

4. **Authenticity check:** List moments when you felt your most authentic self while communicating

5. **Voice description:** Based on your reflections, draft a brief description of your unique voice

You can do this exercise on a piece of paper, or if you'd like to download a digital version of this worksheet, scan the QR code below:

Authenticity as your compass

Objective: To ensure your voice remains authentic and true to yourself.

Authenticity is key to making a genuine connection with your audience. Writing as you speak helps maintain this authenticity, making your message relatable and engaging.

1. **Speak your mind:** Record yourself explaining your book's concept as if to a friend. Transcribe this.

2. **Language analysis:** Highlight phrases that feel particularly 'you' and list why.

3. **Authenticity reflection:** Identify any parts that feel forced or inauthentic.

4. **Adjustment plan:** Make changes to align more closely with your authentic voice.

5. **Gathering feedback:** Share your adjusted feedback explanation with a friend or mentor for feedback on authenticity.

You can do this exercise on a piece of paper, or if you'd like to download a digital version of this worksheet, scan the QR code below:

Voice guideline creation

Objective: To develop a guideline outlining the tone, style and language to be used for your brand.

Step 1: Define Your Brand Identity

1. Mission and Vision: Clearly articulate your brand's mission and vision. What do you aim to achieve, and how do you want to be perceived?
2. Core Values: List the core values that define your brand. These values will heavily influence your tone and style.

Step 2: Identify Your Audience

1. Target Audience: Define who your primary audience is. Consider demographics, interests, and pain points.
2. Audience Preferences: Research the preferred communication styles of your audience. What resonates with them? Formal or informal language? Professional or casual tone?

Step 3: Analyse Competitors and Industry Leaders

1. Competitor Analysis: Look at how your competitors communicate. Identify what works well and what doesn't.
2. Industry Best Practices: Study the communication styles of industry leaders. Take note of effective strategies that align with your brand.

Step 4: Establish Your Tone

1. Adjectives and Descriptions: Choose adjectives that describe your brand's tone (e.g., friendly, professional, authoritative, witty).
2. Do's and Don'ts: Create a list of do's and don'ts for your tone. For example, do be conversational, don't use jargon.

Step 5: Develop Your Style

1. Formality Level: Decide the level of formality your writing should have. This could range from highly formal to very casual.
2. Sentence Structure: Define the preferred sentence structure. Short and concise, or more descriptive and elaborate?
3. Vocabulary and Language: Decide on the type of vocabulary and language. Simple and straightforward, or complex and technical?

Step 6: Create Style Guidelines

1. Grammar and Punctuation: Set rules for grammar and punctuation. Will you follow AP Style, Chicago Manual of Style, or something else?
2. Voice: Decide if your voice is going to be first person, second person, or third person.
3. Consistency: Ensure consistency in spelling, capitalization, and other stylistic elements.

Step 7: Incorporate Brand Elements

1. Taglines and Slogans: Include any taglines or slogans that should be used consistently.
2. Key Messages: Define key messages that should be communicated consistently across all writing.

Step 8: Provide Examples

1. Positive Examples: Provide examples of writing that align with your guidelines.
2. Negative Examples: Show examples of what not to do, highlighting why they don't align with your guidelines.

Step 9: Create a Review Process

1. Peer Review: Establish a process for peer reviewing content to ensure it meets the guidelines.
2. Feedback Loop: Create a feedback loop for continuous improvement of the guidelines.

Step 10: Document and Distribute

1. Documentation: Compile all the guidelines into a comprehensive document.
2. Training: Provide training for team members to ensure they understand and can effectively implement the guidelines.
3. Accessibility: Make the document easily accessible to anyone who needs it.

Step 11: Periodic Review and Update

1. Regular Updates: Schedule regular reviews of the guidelines to ensure they remain relevant and effective.
2. Incorporate Feedback: Adjust the guidelines based on feedback from the team and changes in the industry or audience preferences.

You can do this exercise on a piece of paper, or if you'd like to download a digital version of this worksheet, scan the QR code below:

Consistency across platforms

Objective: To maintain a consistent voice across all platforms.

A consistent voice across your book, blog, social media and public speaking engagements enhances your brand and makes your message recognisable.

1. **Voice guideline creation:** Develop a guideline outlining your tone, style and language.
2. **Cross-platform analysis:** Review your content across different platforms for voice consistency.
3. **Adjustment actions:** Identify discrepancies and plan adjustments for consistency.
4. **Implementation:** Apply adjustments and review the impact on audience engagement.
5. **Regular review:** Schedule periodic reviews of your content to ensure ongoing consistency.

You can do this exercise on a piece of paper, or if you'd like to download a digital version of this worksheet, scan the QR code below:

Cultivating your voice through practice

Objective: To refine and evolve your voice through continual writing and feedback.

Practice and experimentation are vital in developing your voice. Encourage feedback and try different writing formats to discover and strengthen your voice.

1. **Daily writing practice:** Commit to writing daily, focusing on expressing your ideas authentically.
2. **Format experimentation:** Try writing in various formats (blogs, social media posts, articles) each week.
3. **Feedback loop:** Share your writings with a trusted circle (such as our online Authority Through Authorship community) for constructive feedback.
4. **Reflection and adjustment:** Reflect on feedback and adjust your writing approach accordingly.
5. **Voice evolution log:** Keep a log of how your voice changes and grows over time.

You can do this exercise on a piece of paper, or if you'd like to download a digital version of this worksheet, scan the QR code below:

CHAPTER 19

DONE IS BETTER THAN PERFECT

You're a busy human. Me, too. The good news is that you don't have to write a 1,000-page book for it to be effective. You also don't have to take three months out of your life to retreat to a cabin in the woods, typewriter in tow, and pensively gaze at the surrounding serenity to write your bestseller. Done is better than perfect and, trust me, it pains me to write that because I am a recovering perfectionist, too.

You must allow yourself to do your first bad draft and get it out there as soon as possible. I call it the first bad draft for a reason. If you position it that way in your mind, you are giving yourself permission for it not to be perfect. It never will be perfect. But it will be done, and it will be generating leads within days or weeks if you do it right.

Additionally, take note that this book is not a chunky monkey. It doesn't need to be to deliver value and do what you came here to do. When I was getting feedback from my coach while writing, he wrote back on Voxer asking, 'Just confirming there are 2 pages for Chapter 2?' Yes, only two pages. I'm not overthinking it. I'm just sharing what I know in the most effective way possible and moving on.

Efficient and effective is the name of the game here.

The primary purpose of writing a book for your business is to provide value to your audience. Whether you're sharing your expertise, solving a problem or offering valuable insights, your book's content is what matters most. Instead of obsessing over perfection, focus on delivering that value as soon as possible.

By adopting the 'Done' mindset, you can get your book into the hands of your audience sooner, helping them address their pain points, answer their questions, and improve their lives. Remember, your readers are looking for solutions not perfection.

Additionally, rather than waiting for the perfect moment or a flawless manuscript, launch your book and start gathering feedback. Your book is a powerful conversation starter. It acts as a gateway to engage with your audience on a deeper level. Developing it quickly allows you to initiate those conversations sooner, building relationships and trust with your readers. This can provide valuable insights, helping you refine your content and tailor your offerings to their needs.

In the fast-paced world of entrepreneurship, time is a precious resource. Waiting for perfection (which, by the way, doesn't exist) or the right time (it will never be the right time) can lead to missed opportunities, especially in a competitive market. Your competitors are also working hard to capture your target audience's attention. Don't let them beat you to it.

Are you sceptical about whether a short book, written over a few days or weeks, has the power to truly move strangers into hot, pre-qualified, ready-to-buy dream clients?

Let me blow that negative attitude right out of the water.

Success #1

The Elements of Style by William Strunk Jr and E. B. White
128 pages

This concise guide to English grammar and writing styles has been a classic since its publication in 1959. It's a go-to reference for writers and has sold millions of copies. Many educational institutions, from elementary schools to universities, have adopted the book as a standard text for lessons in writing and composition. It is often required reading in English and writing courses. One of the book's strengths is its brevity and straightforward advice. It provides practical rules and examples that writers can easily apply to improve their writing. It is still ranking number one in multiple categories as I write this, 64 years later.

Success #2

The Art of War by Sun Tzu
78 pages

This ancient Chinese text on military strategy and tactics is concise but highly influential. It was written more than 2,500 years ago, has been translated into numerous languages and has a global readership. The book has been used not only in the military but also in business and leadership contexts, with executives and entrepreneurs turning to Sun Tzu's words for guidance in navigating the complexities of corporate competition. References to *The Art of War* can be found in movies, books and various other forms of media.

Success #3

Think & Grow Rich by Napolean Hill
320 pages

This book is considered one of the most successful and influential self-help and personal development books of all time. First published in 1937, it has since sold more than 100 million copies worldwide and still holds poll position on bestseller lists decades after its first publication. Countless entrepreneurs, artists and individuals also credit this book as the driving force behind their success.

Success #4

***The Power of Habit* by Charles Duhigg**
400 pages

This book spent a considerable time on The New York Times bestseller list, meaning it was super popular and sold a lot of copies. Duhigg's exploration of the science behind habits and how they can be changed is both informative and accessible. It's a relatively short book that has had a big impact on personal development literature.

Success #5

***The Life-Changing Magic of Tidying Up* by Marie Kondo**
256 pages

Marie Kondo's book on decluttering and organising is short but effective. Within the pages, Kondo introduces the KonMari method. This system encourages people to declutter their homes by keeping only the items that 'spark joy' and to organise their belongings in a specific way. It has become a global phenomenon, inspiring many to declutter their homes and lives. An entire Netflix series was born from this book, first airing in January 2019. The show further increased Kondo's visibility and introduced her ideas to an even broader audience.

Success #6

***Who Moved My Cheese?* by Spencer Johnson**
96 pages

Managerial strategies and personnel administration were never the same after this book was published in 1998. The book is a motivational business fable that uses a simple allegory to convey important lessons about dealing with change and adapting to new circumstances in both personal and professional life. I remember reading this book when I was around 17 years old. The influence of this book continues to resonate throughout the framework of major corporations and has generated hundreds of millions of dollars for Johnson.

As you can see, whether your book is less than 100 pages, a bit less or a bit more, it doesn't matter. Delivering value is the only thing that matters. The length of your book has no influence on the impact it can have.

Every one of the above five books has left a profound impact on countless individuals. Each of them has reshaped the perspectives of their readers, fostering transformation and inspiration. The great news for you is that amassing a fortune doesn't demand swaying millions. By setting your prices strategically, you only need to sway a small number of people each month.

Now you may be thinking, 'That's great Tarryn, but what about the humungous tomes of Tony Robbins and Tim Ferriss? Their books are way bigger than 78 pages.'

Yes, they are but let me point out this vital fact − non-fiction readers want short reads. Think about the way that you read non-fiction books. Are you content to sit down for days and months within your busy schedule to consume practical, non-fiction advice? I bet not. It's why platforms such as Blinkist have become so popular.

Blinkist boasts an impressive user base exceeding 23 million people, each subscribing to a monthly service that distils non-fiction books to their essential insights, offering both audio and print formats directly to your mobile device. Every month, Blinkist introduces 50 new works of non-fiction to its collection. People have short attention spans and want to know what they need to know − yesterday.

If, like me, you know that one day you want to write a much bigger book, then you can. But for now, at this stage of your life, a short book is your ticket forward. Get your dream clients to consume your wisdom as fast as possible, start growing your business and start changing lives.

And if you simply can't let go of the perfectionist tendencies, hear this: once a book is published, you can add to it and change it later. Nothing is set in stone anymore.

Done is better than perfect.

"

In business, perfection is the enemy of profitability.

MARK CUBAN

BUSINESSMAN, INVESTOR, FILM PRODUCER
AND TV PERSONALITY

CHAPTER 20

HOW TO GET INSTANT TRACTION

It's time to get writing. This moment, right here, marks the spot in your life where you decide to take action and do away with those outdated marketing strategies and develop a bountiful, self-fulfilling spring of leads ready to buy from you, and start enjoying your business and life again or even more than you do now. I'm so freaking excited for you!

Before embarking on this transformative journey together, I want to have a heart-to-heart conversation about the passion and determination that has brought you here.

Picture the excitement you're feeling right now – the anticipation, motivation, that sense of *Am I really doing this?* I want you to carry that enthusiasm with you throughout the rest of this book, when you join the free Authority Through Authorship community, as you write your first book, and potential future ones.

Let's not sugar-coat it. This journey won't always be a walk in the park, or it will if it's like those times in the park where you step in dog poop, see your child fall over and scrape a knee and then yell bloody murder at the top of their lungs, as it starts to rain and you see your nightmare ex approaching along the path. You know what I mean.

There will be challenges, moments when you'll need to summon your inner strength, push yourself beyond your limits, and venture into uncharted territory. However, here's a secret shared by all successful authors – write something every day.

In difficult moments, I want you to remember this. You are coura-geous. You are determined. You are equipped with the qualities neces-sary to craft an extraordinary book and design a life filled with impact, passion, inspiration and fulfilment. A life that makes you genuinely say, 'I am so thankful for the life I've created.'

Now, it's time for you to make a commitment to yourself and to this process. Promise yourself to put pen to paper, do the work, and persist until every chapter is completed, your manuscript is finished, and you're launching a book that not only will transform your life but will have a last-ing impact on countless others.

I challenge you to jump in with both feet, embrace the work, diligently follow the roadmap laid out within these pages, and commit to yourself repeatedly because you deserve to cross that finish line. I have unwaver-ing faith that you will.

By picking up this book and investing in your dreams, you're declaring to yourself, 'I'm going to make this work!'

Writing a book is undeniably hard work, but the reward is immea-surable. If, at any point in this journey, self-doubt or imposter syndrome creeps in, rest assured that we will obliterate it. We are arming you with the tools and roadmap necessary to embark on this writing adventure wholeheartedly.

Use the community as your support system. Let it remind you of your strength and resilience. Remember, you are not alone. I am here and so is my team. We're not just providing the tools, we're offering encour-agement and support and reminding you that you can conquer the chal-lenges and accomplish hard things.

It's the challenges that make us stronger and increase our confi-dence, enabling us to make a more significant impact in this world.

So, are you ready to show up for your dreams?

Are you ready to commit to yourself?

Are you ready to commit finally to writing that book?

I'm here with you every step of the way, excited to reach the final page together. In the upcoming chapters, I'll unveil the exact roadmap that will guide us on this incredible journey, but before I do, I want to offer a heartfelt invitation.

Nothing great is ever achieved alone. I want you to join me, my team and entrepreneurial authors who are either just like you or completely different but definitely worth knowing, over in our author community. Inside you will find community support, exclusive content, and early bird alerts on industry news and events. To join this free community, scan the QR code below.

Get excited, and I'll see you there.

"

Vision without traction
is merely hallucination.

GINO WICKMAN

AUTHOR, SPEAKER, TEACHER, AND ENTREPRENEUR

CHAPTER 21

THE ART OF STORYTELLING

Storytelling sells. It is that simple. If you want to stand out from the crowd and make your ideal clients feel you are speaking directly to them, you need to become a master storyteller. You can develop a relationship with them from the pages of your book and turn them into pre-qualified leads without having to hop on a sales call. In this chapter, I show you how to master the art of storytelling that sells.

In the vast landscape of business and marketing, where every entrepreneur is vying for attention, storytelling is a potent tool that has the ability to cut through the noise and leave an indelible mark on the minds of your audience. It's not just a creative endeavour, it's a strategic weapon that can connect with your audience on a profound level, elevate your brand and ultimately drive sales.

Unveiling the narrative landscape

Imagine you're not just telling a story or writing a book; you're crafting an emotional roller-coaster. Buckle up because we're about to dive into the heart of what makes a tale truly captivating.

Picture your audience not as passive listeners but as eager participants in this grand narrative. We're not just throwing facts and figures at them, we're inviting them on an emotional journey, a ride that'll make them laugh, maybe shed a tear, and ultimately nod with a sense of fulfilment and a sigh of 'Ahhhh, this person gets me!'

At the core of it all, the type of story we need to write isn't just a string of events or boring (useful as they may be) facts – it's an adventure, a thrill, a roller-coaster of feelings. People crave more than data or information. They hunger for an experience that tugs at their heartstrings. We're not in the business of simply storytelling – we're in the business of weaving dreams, of creating moments that resonate.

Your ideal clients aren't just observers, they are the heroes or heroines of this tale. They're not merely reading about challenges and triumphs, they're living them. They're facing down obstacles, conquering fears, and standing tall at the end. It's a visceral connection that goes beyond words and numbers – it's an emotional symphony.

A well-crafted narrative isn't just a set of instructions, it's a mirror reflecting your client as the protagonist. The clients should be able to see themselves in the story, navigating through highs and lows just like they do in real life. It's about making them feel seen, understood and, ultimately, victorious.

As you write, let's not just string sentences together, but create a world where your client is a player rather than just a spectator. Let's make them feel the highs, the lows and everything in between. Because in the end, it's not just about conveying information – it's about forging a connection, a bond that transcends the boundaries of mere words and numbers. It's about making your client the hero or heroine of a story that's uniquely theirs.

Crafting your brand saga

Your brand is more than just a logo or a tagline. It's a living, breathing entity with a story waiting to be told. Through your book, you must create a brand saga that captivates and compels. Whether you're a seasoned pro in the business world or you're just starting to dip your toes into the entrepreneurial waters, there's something magical about understanding the soul of your brand story. It's like figuring out the 'why' behind what you do.

What are the values that fuel your business engine? What hurdles have you faced, and how did you conquer them like a superhero?

Now this might sound a bit too poetic for the business scene, but bear with me. When you start unravelling the layers of your brand narrative, you're not just sharing facts and figures, you're sharing a piece of yourself, your journey and your vision. It's the kind of stuff that builds trust between you and your customers, and creates a genuine connection. It's like inviting people to sit around a virtual campfire and swap stories.

You're not just selling a product or a service, you're inviting people to join an expedition, to be a part of something bigger. You're not hiding the rough patches but proudly showcasing the battle scars because, let's be real, every success story has a few setbacks in the mix.

And here's the real kicker – by answering these questions about your brand, you're not just building trust, you're turning your audience into participants in your journey. It's not a one-sided conversation where you're shouting about your greatness, it's a dialogue, an exchange of stories and values.

By sharing the real, raw and vulnerable parts of who you are, you allow people a look behind the curtain they so desperately crave. In fact, they need to see those parts to trust you fully, to lean into what you have to say, and to get to know you without ever actually meeting you. Ultimately people do business with other people, so let them see you, warts and all!

Now if this brings up fear in you, know that this is normal. We are hardwired to want to be accepted by the tribe and it is natural to be scared of baring the 'not-so-put-together' version of you lest the world ends and you wind up living in a box, a disgrace to everything and everyone you hold dear. (At least that was the narrative that played out for me when I first tried to connect genuinely beyond the safety of my polished brand.)

I promise it gets easier and is so, so worth it. It's the ultimate freedom and the key to unlocking more joy within your business. It's like a pheromone perfume that has your dream clients practically stampeding to work with you.

Whether you're a business veteran who's been around the block or a fresh-faced startup eager to make your mark, it's important to understand that your brand is not just a logo, it's a living, breathing entity with a story yearning to be shared. It is part of who you are. And, in the grand scheme of things, your brand saga might just be the captivating narrative that sets you apart in the bustling marketplace. So, spill the beans, share your victories, embrace your challenges and let your brand story become the heartbeat of your business.

Still quivering at the very idea? Here's some more convincing for you … because we're doing this.

Connecting on a human level

In the age of digital communication, it's easy to lose touch with the human side of business. Storytelling, however, is a bridge that spans the gap, connecting you with your clients on a human level. Sharing your own struggles and triumphs can create a sense of empathy and relatability. We're not just talking about any stories; we're talking about the power of vulnerability and authenticity.

It's like opening a treasure chest of realness and letting your clients peek inside. You, the brave, put-together, successful businessperson, are sharing the struggles you faced and the triumphs you celebrated. It's like pulling back the curtain and revealing the person behind the polished facade.

Why is this so important? The answer is simple – it creates a sense of empathy and relatability. When you lay your cards on the table, sharing not only your successes but also the hurdles you had to leap over, your clients nod their heads and think, 'Hey, they're just like me.' It's a powerful realisation that transforms your business relationship from a transactional exchange into a genuine connection.

Think of your story as a mirror, reflecting the experiences and aspirations of your audience. As audience members read or listen, they see fragments of their own journey reflected back at them. It's a powerful moment of recognition that goes beyond products and services. It's about shared humanity.

So, the next time you're tempted to bash out a generic-sounding chapter, send out a robotic-sounding email or generate a basic social media post, consider weaving a bit of your story into the narrative. It doesn't have to be an epic saga. It could be a snippet, a moment or a lesson learned. Your clients will appreciate the authenticity. In return, you'll find a bridge forming – a bridge built on shared stories, vulnerability and the wonderfully messy tapestry of what it means to be human in this digital age.

Speak directly to your ideal client

Imagine walking into a cosy coffee shop with a friend, ready to share the latest happenings in your life. You settle into a comfy chair with the aroma of freshly brewed coffee enveloping you. As your friend leans in, genuinely interested, you feel a sense of connection, knowing they truly understand you.

Now, let's bring that warm, comforting feeling into the world of storytelling that sells. Think of yourself not just as a seller but as that attentive friend eager to hear your ideal client's story. Your product or service becomes the supporting character in their narrative, addressing the client's struggles, wishes and aspirations.

It's like tailoring a bespoke suit by considering every curve and contour. You delve into their psyche, recognise their pain points, and acknowledge the challenges the client faces. It's not simply about using your words to showcase what you're selling, it's about creating a conversation that resonates with your reader on a personal level.

Through the art of storytelling, you're not just presenting facts and features, you're crafting a vivid scenario. You're setting the scene where your client envisions a brighter future, one where your offering plays a crucial role in their success story.

Think about it as a movie plot where your client is the protagonist, facing obstacles and seeking solutions but ultimately triumphing with your product or service. Your words become the screenplay, weaving a tale that captures their attention and stirs their emotions.

In this narrative, you're not just a seller, but a trusted confidante, a guide on the journey. The client sees you as someone who gets him or her, who understands the nuances of the challenges. It's like having a GPS that not only provides directions but also understands the destination's significance.

When your client feels seen and heard in this way, a powerful transformation occurs. You're not just selling a product or service; you're offering a solution that aligns with their deepest needs. They're not just making a purchase; they're investing in a relationship built on trust and understanding.

The next time you step into the role of a storyteller in the realm of selling (such as when you are writing your book), remember the coffee shop metaphor. Create an atmosphere where your client feels like they're having a meaningful conversation with a friend. Tailor your narrative to be as comforting and relatable as that cosy chair in the coffee shop.

Watch as your ideal client not only hears your story but becomes an active participant. This means they take action and either help themself and become a huge fan or become a paying client as well as a fan who, when telling their own success tale, will sing your praises to anyone and everyone within earshot.

The art of compelling calls to action

Imagine you're wrapping up the section of your journey through the world of communication and persuasion and putting the finishing touches on each chapter of the book you've so carefully crafted to keep your readers hooked. Now...it's time to talk about weaving storytelling into your calls to action. It's not just about wrapping things up neatly, it's about setting the stage for what comes next, such as buying your next-level offers.

Think of it like the cliffhanger at the end of your favourite TV show which leaves you eager for the next one. You don't want your audience to close the book, you want them to turn the page and dive into the next chapter, and onto the next level of your entrepreneurial world.

Crafting a compelling narrative is like planting the seeds of curiosity and excitement. Your story doesn't stop, it nudges your audience to step into the spotlight and become the heroes or heroines of the next scene. You're not just asking them to click a button or make a purchase, but inviting them to join in, to be a part of something bigger.

This is about turning a simple call to action into an irresistible invitation. It's not just about selling a product; it's about inviting your ideal client to become a character in the story you're narrating. It's like saying, 'Hey, don't just buy this, let's create something together. Let's build a narrative where you're not just a consumer but a crucial part of the plot of your own transformation and success.'

As you wrap up this chapter, remember that your story doesn't end when the reader finishes it – it evolves. Your book won't be a full stop but a comma leading to the next adventure. Your call to action isn't a demand of your reader but an invitation to your client to embark on a journey together, where you are turning casual observers into active participants in the tale you're telling.

In the end, it's not just about closing deals but about building connections and co-authoring a story that leaves everyone excitedly waiting for the next page to turn.

"

Marketing is no longer about the stuff that you make, but about the stories you tell.

SETH GODIN

ENTREPRENEUR, AUTHOR AND SPEAKER

Brand saga development

Objective: To reflect on, and dive deep into the story of your brand.

Section 1: Discover Your Brand's Core

1. Your Brand's Genesis:

    - What inspired you to start your business?
    - Describe the moment or event that sparked the creation of your brand.

2. Mission and Vision:

    - What is your brand's mission statement?
    - What vision do you have for the future of your brand?

3. Core Values:

    - List the top five values that your brand embodies.
    - How do these values influence your business decisions?

4. Unique Value Proposition:

    - What sets your brand apart from competitors?
    - What unique value do you offer to your customers?

Section 2: Mapping the Journey

1. Challenges and Triumphs:

    - What significant obstacles has your brand overcome?
    - Describe how you addressed these challenges creatively.

2. Milestones:

- Identify key milestones in your brand's history.
- How have these milestones shaped your brand's trajectory?

3. Lessons Learned:

- What are the most valuable lessons you've learned from running your brand?
- How have these insights shaped your approach to business?

Section 3: Engaging the Audience

1. Storytelling Elements:

- Identify stories from your brand's journey that exemplify your core values.
- How can these stories be told to resonate emotionally with your audience?

2. Creating Connections:

- What methods will you use to share these stories? (e.g., social media, blogs, podcasts)
- How will you encourage audience interaction and feedback?

3. Building Trust:

- How will you showcase the authentic, vulnerable aspects of your brand?
- What strategies will you implement to build trust and foster loyalty among your customers?

Section 4: Visual and Verbal Identity

1. Brand Voice:

   - How would you describe your brand's voice (e.g., professional, friendly, authoritative)?
   - Provide examples of how this voice is used in your communications.

2. Visual Identity:

   - What are the key elements of your brand's visual style (e.g., colours, logo, typography)?
   - How do these elements reflect your brand's personality and values?

Section 5: Reflection and Adaptation

1. Feedback Loop:

   - How will you gather and utilize customer feedback to improve your brand?
   - What mechanisms will you put in place to ensure continuous learning and adaptation?

2. Future Planning:

   - What are your long-term goals for your brand?
   - How will you continue to evolve and remain relevant in your market?

3. Fear and Challenges:

   - What fears do you have about sharing your brand's story?

- How can you address these fears to move forward confidently?

You can do this exercise on a piece of paper, or if you'd like to download a digital version of this worksheet, scan the QR code below:

SECTION 4

PUBLISHING PATHWAYS

CHAPTER 22

EDITING AND PROOFREADING
Polishing Your Manuscript

Even though this book is more about writing your own book within 28 days, I couldn't help but add a little extra to help you start thinking about the publishing process. Over the next few chapters, I'll give you a brief overview of what to consider and expect when you move your manuscript from the writing to the publishing stage.

The journey of writing your book does not end with completion of the first draft. It transitions into a crucial phase of refinement. Editing and proofreading are the fine-tuning processes that elevate your manuscript from good to exceptional.

This chapter is dedicated to guiding you through these stages, ensuring your book is clear, coherent and error-free, reflecting the high standards of your expertise and authority.

The difference between editing and proofreading

Editing and proofreading serve different but complementary purposes. Editing focuses on the content, structure, clarity and style of your manuscript. It involves rephrasing sentences for better flow, restructuring paragraphs for coherence, and ensuring your arguments are persuasive and logically presented.

Proofreading, on the other hand, is the final step before publication, concentrating on surface errors such as grammar, spelling, punctuation and formatting inconsistencies. Both stages are essential to producing a polished, professional book.

I encourage you to get your editing done by professionals and not by your friends or yourself, even if they, or you, happen to be exceptionally good at English (or whatever language you are writing in).

I have seen too many manuscripts come across my desk that have been edited by well-meaning friends (not professionals in the art of structural editing, copy editing or proofreading), and we have had to do a full re-edit of the manuscript. Don't let that be your story.

The editing process: content and structure

Start with a high-level content edit (also known as a structural edit), assessing your manuscript for clarity of argument, relevance of content, and narrative engagement. Does each chapter serve the purpose of your book's core message? Are there redundant sections that could be removed or areas that need further development?

This stage may involve significant rewriting or reorganisation of sections to enhance the flow of information and ensure that your book is compelling and easy to follow.

Style and voice consistency

During the editing phase, your editor will pay close attention to maintaining a consistent style and voice throughout your manuscript. This consistency reinforces your unique brand and makes your book more enjoyable to read. Ensure that your editor understands your voice and your goals for the book, so their suggestions enhance rather than dilute your personal style.

Engaging a professional editor

While self-editing is an important part of the process, I believe that hiring a professional editor is a must. A professional editor can provide a new perspective and expertise that elevate your manuscript. They can identify weaknesses you might overlook, offer suggestions to improve readability and engagement and ensure your book meets industry standards.

Choose an editor with experience in your genre or field and be open to their feedback – it's an investment in the quality of your book.

The proofreading stage

Proofreading should be the final step before your book goes to print or is published online. It's best conducted on a formatted (also known as a typeset) version of your manuscript, as this can reveal errors that may not be obvious in a word-processing document.

If possible, hire a professional proofreader to catch mistakes you and your editor may have missed. Remember, even minor errors can detract from your credibility as an author and authority in your field.

Using beta readers

Before finalising your manuscript, consider sharing it with beta readers. Choose individuals from your target audience or peers in your field who can provide valuable feedback on your content, clarity, engagement and overall impact. Beta readers can also catch overlooked errors, ensuring your book is polished from both a content and technical standpoint.

Implementing feedback

As you receive feedback from editors, proofreaders and beta readers, carefully consider each suggestion. Not all feedback will align with your vision for your book but you should remain open to changes that enhance its quality. Implementing these suggestions thoughtfully will refine your manuscript into a polished, professional book of which you can be proud.

Editing and proofreading are critical stages in the book-writing process, transforming your manuscript into a polished, professional work. They require patience, attention to detail and a willingness to accept and integrate feedback.

By dedicating the necessary time and resources to these stages, you ensure your book reflects the highest standards of excellence, reinforcing your position as an authority in your field and enhancing the impact on your readers and your business.

"

The secret to editing your work is simple: you need to become its reader instead of its writer.

ZADIE SMITH

ENGLISH NOVELIST, ESSAYIST
AND SHORT STORY WRITER

CHAPTER 23

DESIGN AND FORMATTING
Making Your Book Visually Appealing

Truth be told, anyone can throw a book up on Amazon these days, but producing a book that is poor quality will damage your brand and reputation rather than enhancing it. Your book's visual appeal plays a crucial role in capturing and retaining your readers' interest. It's not just the cover that matters but also the internal design and formatting that will help to make your book a pleasure to read.

We've all had the experience of ignoring a book on the shelf because of the dodgy cover design, or the unpleasant experience of trying to read a book that looks like a toddler tried to do it for art time. But that's not going to be your book because you, savvy entrepreneur, understand the importance of quality, right!?

This chapter will guide you through the process of designing and formatting your book to enhance readability, emphasise key points and reflect the professional quality of your content.

The importance of professional design

First impressions count, and your cover design is often the first thing a reader will notice. Think of it as the shop front or professional face of your business. A professionally designed cover communicates the value and seriousness of your work, encouraging potential readers to take a closer look. The internal layout is equally important, as it affects the reader's experience, engagement and comprehension.

Investing in professional design services can significantly elevate the perceived value of your book and place you above the competition.

Cover design: capturing the essence

Your cover should be a visual representation of your book's core message. It needs to be eye-catching, relevant and aligned with your branding. Consider your target audience and what visual elements would resonate with them. For the love of all that is holy, please ensure that you research what is selling well. Just because you find something visually appealing, doesn't mean everyone else does. A good cover designer will be able to translate your book's essence into a compelling visual that stands out in a crowded marketplace.

Typography and readability

The choice of fonts and typography within your book is vital for readability. Nobody wants to squint at a page or feel like they are reading a children's book. Body text should be easy on the eyes, with headings and subheadings clearly differentiated to guide the reader through the content. Avoid the temptation to use too many font styles because this can create visual confusion. Your designer can help you select a combination that reflects your book's tone while ensuring a smooth reading experience.

Layout and spacing

A well-thought-out layout makes your book more engaging and user-friendly. Elements like margins, line spacing and paragraph indentation may seem minor but they have a significant impact on the reader's comfort and ability to absorb information.

Features such as bullet points, numbered lists, and block quotes can break up text and highlight important information, making your content more digestible.

Incorporating visual elements

Diagrams, charts, tables and images can enrich your content, illustrating complex ideas in a straightforward visual manner. These elements should be professionally designed and clearly labelled, with captions that explain their relevance to the text.

Remember to consider the formatting requirements of different publishing platforms, especially if you plan to release print and digital versions of your book. Also be aware that the more visual elements you include, the more it will cost you to print, thereby eating into your profit margin or forcing you to list your book as more expensive than your competitors.

Consistency across chapters

Maintain consistency in design and formatting choices throughout your book. This consistency reinforces your brand and helps create a cohesive reading experience. Elements such as chapter titles, headings and footers should follow a uniform style, contributing to the book's professional appearance.

Navigational aids

Features like a table of contents, index and glossary not only add to the professional quality of your book but also make it more user-friendly. They allow readers to navigate your content and reference specific information easily, enhancing the usability and value of your book.

Not all books need an index or glossary but if your topic uses lots of jargon or unfamiliar words that just cannot be avoided then consider including these.

Check before you release

Before finalising your design and formatting and media launch, ensure you order a print-proof copy of your book to look over. This can be a digital copy or a physical proof (honestly, I would check both), allowing you to review the design in the format your readers will experience it.

Pay attention to details like the alignment of text and images, the quality of visual elements and the overall aesthetic appeal. This step is crucial for catching any errors or inconsistencies that could detract from your book's impact.

Design and formatting are not just about aesthetics. They are about creating a reading experience that complements and enhances your content. A well-designed book invites readers in, makes the journey through your content enjoyable and leaves a lasting impression of professionalism and authority.

By focusing on these visual elements, you ensure your book is not only informative but also visually engaging, further establishing your expertise and enhancing your brand.

"

A parent or a teacher has only his lifetime; a good book can teach forever.

LOUIS L'ARMOUR

AMERICAN NOVELIST AND SHORT STORY WRITER

CHAPTER 24

PUBLISHING OPTIONS

The journey from manuscript to published book is filled with critical decisions. One of the most significant is how to publish your work. This chapter will navigate the landscape of publishing options, examining the pros and cons of traditional publishing versus self-publishing and hybrid publishing. This will help you make an informed decision that aligns with your goals, resources and aspirations as an author and entrepreneur.

Traditional publishing:
the perceived path of prestige and support

Traditional publishing involves partnering with established publishing houses that take on the responsibility of editing, designing, marketing and distributing your book. This path offers several advantages:

- **Credibility and prestige:** Being published by a recognised publishing house can significantly enhance both your book's credibility and your own.
- **Professional editing and design services:** Publishers provide professional editing, design and formatting services, ensuring your book meets industry standards.
- **Marketing and distribution support:** They also handle marketing and have established channels for distribution, both online and in brick-and-mortar stores.

However, traditional publishing also has drawbacks:

- **Competitive and time-consuming:** Getting a publishing deal can be highly competitive, requiring approaching agents and facing potential rejections. Even after securing a deal, the time to publication can be lengthy.
- **Less control:** Authors often have limited control, if any, over the book's final appearance and marketing strategy. If you want to understand what this may look like, then I encourage you to watch season 5 of *'Workin' Moms'*, which can be found on Netflix.
- **Reduced royalties:** Royalties from traditional publishing are typically lower than self-publishing, with authors receiving a smaller percentage of sales. Rates vary. However, you can expect to receive only 5–15 percent back on the sale of each book.
- **The smoke and mirrors of advances:** Many think that using a traditional publisher means getting paid to write their book. Some publishing houses pay authors an 'advance' to write their books. The key word to note here is 'advance'. Yes, this means that the author receives some money from the publisher to write, but then the author doesn't see a cent of royalty payments after the book has been published until that advance amount has been paid back in full.
- **Just a number:** Many of my authors who have previously published with traditional publishing houses have reported feeling unsupported and like they were just a number. It is common for authors not to receive any support at all in the writing process. This means that many have to hire a book coach to get the manuscript to a point that the publishing house deems acceptable.

Self-publishing: control, speed and higher royalties

Self-publishing puts you in the driver's seat, allowing you to publish your book on your own terms. This approach has gained popularity for several reasons:

- **Complete control:** You maintain control over your book's content, design, pricing and marketing strategy.
- **Higher royalties:** Self-published authors can earn higher royalties per book sold, especially through digital platforms.
- **Speed to market:** Without traditional publishing gatekeepers, you can bring your book to market much faster.

The challenges of self-publishing include:

- **Upfront costs:** You bear the upfront costs for editing, design, formatting and marketing.
- **Marketing and distribution efforts:** Without the support of a publishing house, the responsibility of marketing and distributing your book falls on you.
- **Quality and credibility challenges:** Ensuring your book matches the quality of traditionally published books requires significant effort. Self-published books may face more scrutiny from readers and retailers.
- **Time drain:** If you choose to self-publish, you will be responsible for navigating the complex world of writing, publishing and marketing a book, and finding and coordinating all the specialists required to help produce a quality book that enhances your brand and business.

Making the decision

Choosing between traditional and self-publishing depends on your priorities.

- **For authors seeking prestige and support:** If the prestige of a publishing house and support in editing, design, and marketing are paramount, and you're willing to navigate the competitive landscape, traditional publishing might be the right path.
- **For authors valuing control and speed:** If maintaining control over every aspect of your book and bringing it to market quickly are your primary goals, self-publishing offers the freedom and flexibility to achieve this.

Hybrid publishing – a middle ground

But wait! There is another option. Hybrid publishing models offer a compromise by blending elements of traditional and self-publishing. These services may provide professional editing and design with more favourable royalty splits than traditional publishing, but often require an investment from the author.

The team and I here at Automatic Authority Publishing & Press House are considered a hybrid publisher. We work closely with our authors to write, publish and market their books. Our authors come to us at various stages in their journey. We take the time to understand their unique goals and vision for their book and then decide if we are a good fit to work together.

We value maintaining our authors' voices and creativity at all times. We consider our job to advise them of the best options based on our expertise. It is then up to them what they choose to do with that advice. Our services include ghost writing, book coaching, publishing, marketing, distribution, public relations (PR) and media services. Oh! And one other thing ... we don't take a cent of your royalties. Every dollar your book earns goes straight back to you.

Aside from our intimate partnership experiences, we also offer self-paced courses and Masterminds.

To find out more about how we work, scan the QR code below:

Ready to become the go-to authority in your field and make your book dreams a reality with the help of the Automatic Authority team? Scan the QR code below to apply:

The decision between traditional, self-publishing and hybrid publishing is significant, shaping your book's journey from manuscript to finding readers. Consider your goals, resources and the level of control you wish to maintain. Regardless of your path, publishing your book is a remarkable achievement, marking your entry into the realm of published authors and further establishing your authority in your field.

"

How you choose to publish your book is up to you. The key consideration is whether that decision will ultimately result in a book that will enhance your brand and not damage it. Only you know the path which is correct for you.

TARRYN REEVES

AUTHOR, SPEAKER AND PUBLISHER

SECTION 5

LAUNCH AND MARKETING MASTERY

CHAPTER 25

LAUNCH STRATEGIES
Building Anticipation and Momentum

Your book's launch is a pivotal moment in your journey as an author. It's an opportunity to make a significant impact, attract attention and start generating sales. A successful launch can propel your book to the top of the charts and solidify your status as an authority in your field.

This chapter is dedicated to crafting an effective launch strategy that builds anticipation, engages your audience and maximises your book's visibility from day one.

Building pre-launch buzz

The groundwork for a successful launch is laid well before the release date. Start building buzz around your book by teasing its content, cover and key takeaways on your social media platforms, blog and newsletter. Share behind-the-scenes glimpses of your writing process, cover design choices and other aspects of the book's journey to publication. This not only engages your existing audience but can also attract new followers curious about your work.

Leveraging your network

Your network is a powerful asset in amplifying your book's launch. Reach out to peers, mentors and influencers within your industry for support.

This can take the form of social media shout-outs, endorsements or invitations to guest post or speak on their platforms.

If you have built relationships with bloggers or podcasters, now is the time to pitch yourself for interviews and features, providing valuable content while promoting your book.

Creating a launch team

A launch team is a group of dedicated fans and supporters who help spread the word about your book in exchange for early access or other incentives. Recruit members from your email list, social media followers and professional contacts. Equip them with promotional materials and clear instructions on how they can help, whether that's posting reviews, talking about the book on social media or telling friends and colleagues.

Using pre-orders

Pre-orders can play a significant role in your book's initial success, boosting its rankings on launch day and providing an early revenue stream. Offer special incentives for pre-orders, such as exclusive content, a companion workbook or access to a private webinar. Make the process easy and enticing, emphasising the benefits of ordering your book ahead of its official release.

We do not use this as part of our usual strategy when working with our intimate partnership clients, but it can be effective. We've never failed to hit a bestseller list for any of our clients, even without pre-orders.

Hosting a launch event

A launch event, whether in-person or virtual, can create significant momentum. An in-person event could be a book signing at a local bookstore or a launch party with a short reading or talk. For a broader reach, consider a virtual launch using platforms like Zoom or Facebook Live to host a Q&A, interview or reading.

Promote your event well in advance and consider partnering with other authors or influencers to expand your audience. We have organised launch events and tours for our authors, and the results have been both phenomenal and fun.

Capitalising on media and press coverage

Reach out to local and industry-specific media outlets with a well-crafted press release highlighting your book's unique aspects and its relevance to current trends or issues. Offer yourself as a source for interviews or articles on topics related to your book's content. Media coverage can significantly increase visibility and credibility.

Monitoring and adjusting your strategy

After your book launches, monitor its performance closely. Pay attention to sales data, reader feedback and online reviews. This information can guide your ongoing marketing efforts, helping you to adjust your strategy as needed to maintain momentum and continue reaching new readers.

A successful book launch is a multifaceted endeavour that requires planning, creativity and engagement. By building anticipation, leveraging your network, utilising pre-orders, and hosting a memorable launch event, you set the stage for success.

Remember, the launch is just the beginning of your book's journey. Continued marketing efforts are crucial for sustaining visibility and impact over time. As we entrepreneurs know, we have to continually market to sell and evolve.

66

Anybody can throw a book up on Amazon, whether or not it sells is a different story. You must let as many people as possible know about your book in order to stand out from the crowd and gain momentum.

TARRYN REEVES

AUTHOR, SPEAKER AND PUBLISHER

CHAPTER 26

MARKETING YOUR BOOK
Tactics for Maximum Exposure

A book's launch is a critical moment, but the work to keep it visible, selling and appealing to new readers continues far beyond. Effective, ongoing marketing ensures your book remains a relevant and desirable resource in your field, helping to grow your business and establish your authority. This chapter outlines strategic marketing tactics to maximise your book's exposure and sustain its success over time.

Leveraging content marketing

Content marketing is a powerful tool for keeping your book in the public eye. Create blog posts, articles, videos and infographics that tie back to your book's themes and key takeaways. This not only provides value to your audience but also keeps your book at the forefront of reader's minds. Guest posting on reputable sites in your industry can also expand your reach and attract readers.

Optimising for Amazon and other online retailers

For many authors, online retailers are a primary sales channel. Optimise your book's listing with compelling descriptions, strategic keywords and high-quality cover images. Encourage satisfied readers to leave reviews. These play a crucial role in a book's visibility and perceived value on platforms like Amazon.

Using email marketing

Your email list is a direct line to your most engaged audience. Regular updates, exclusive content and special promotions related to your book can keep your audience interested and engaged. Segmenting your list allows for more personalised communication, targeting readers with content and offers that match their specific interests and needs.

Engaging with social media

Social media platforms offer a dynamic way to connect with readers and promote your book. Share updates, insights and behind-the-scenes looks at your author journey. Use hashtags strategically to reach a wider audience. Consider running targeted ads to promote your book to specific demographics or interest groups.

Speaking engagements and workshops

Offering to speak at conferences, workshops and other events can significantly boost your book's visibility. These engagements position you as an authority in your field and provide an opportunity to promote your book to an interested audience directly. Virtual webinars or workshops can also reach a wide audience without the geographical constraints of in-person events.

Collaborating with other authors and influencers

Collaborations can introduce your book to new audiences. Look for opportunities to partner with other authors or influencers on projects, interviews or joint promotions that benefit all parties. These partnerships can be particularly effective when the collaborators' audiences share interests with your target readers.

Paid advertising

Paid advertising can be an effective way to boost your book's visibility. Platforms like Amazon Ads, Facebook, Instagram and Google Ads offer targeting options to reach potential readers based on their interests, behaviour and demographics. Start with a small budget to test different strategies. Then refine your approach based on performance.

Regularly review and adjust your strategy

The market is always changing. What works today may not work tomorrow. Regularly review your marketing strategy's performance, experiment with new tactics and adjust your approach based on what is most effective. Stay informed about trends in book marketing and your industry to keep your strategies fresh and relevant.

Marketing your book is an ongoing effort, essential for sustaining its success and leveraging it to grow your business. By employing a mix of content marketing, optimisation, social media engagement, speaking engagements, collaborations and paid advertising, you can keep your book in the spotlight.

Remember, each book has its unique path to success. The key is to remain adaptable, innovative and persistent in your marketing efforts.

> ## "
>
> *Good marketing makes the company look smart. Great marketing makes the customer feel smart.*
>
> **JOE CHERNOV**
>
> MARKETER AND STARTUP ADVISER

CHAPTER 27

LEVERAGING YOUR BOOK TO GROW YOUR BUSINESS AND BRAND

By now, I am sure that you understand that publishing a book is not just an achievement in its own right. It's a powerful tool for business growth and brand development. This chapter explores strategies for leveraging your book to enhance your reputation, attract clients or customers, and open up opportunities for your business.

By integrating your book into your broader business strategy, you can maximise its impact and ensure it serves as a catalyst for success.

Establish your authority and credibility

Your book positions you as an authority in your field, enhancing your credibility with clients, peers and the media. Use this newfound authority to contribute articles to reputable industry publications, speak at conferences and participate in panel discussions. Each opportunity not only reinforces your status as an expert but also brings your book and your business to a wider audience.

Integrate your book into your marketing materials

Your book should be a cornerstone of your marketing efforts. Feature it prominently on your website, in your email signature and on your social media profiles. Create case studies, blog posts and video content that highlight key insights from your book, demonstrating the value it provides and encouraging more people to read the book.

Enhance your website with a dedicated section for your book, including a blog where you can continue to explore its themes, share updates and engage with readers. Embrace video content by creating a YouTube channel or hosting webinars that delve deeper into your book's topics, offering additional insights and value.

Use your book as a lead generation tool

With this, you have a few options. You can offer your book, or parts of it, as a free download or, better yet, offer your book for sale at a small fee built into a full marketing funnel complete with upsells and downsells to skyrocket your business in exchange for email sign-ups on your website.

You will grow your email list (people you can market to on an ongoing basis), provide potential clients with a valuable resource that introduces them to your expertise and approach, and make money while you sleep. Consider creating a series of automated emails based on a prospect's behaviour inside the funnel that delves deeper into the book's topics, thereby nurturing leads and guiding the prospect towards your services or products.

Develop training programs and workshops

Your book's content can be the foundation for training programs, workshops or online courses. These can target individuals or businesses seeking to implement the strategies or solutions you discuss in your book. Not only does this provide another revenue stream, it also further establishes you as the go-to expert in your niche.

Networking and collaborations

The credibility and visibility that come with being a published author can open doors for further networking opportunities and collaborations. Whether it's partnering with other businesses for joint ventures, being invited to join prestigious industry groups or collaborating on projects with peers, your book can be a valuable asset in expanding your professional network.

Cross-promote your services or products

Use your book to cross-promote other services or products offered by your business. Include calls to action within the book itself (like the QR codes you see within this book), directing readers to your website for more information on your consulting services, speaking engagements or other products. This can be an effective way to convert readers into customers or clients.

Collect and leverage testimonials and reviews

Positive reviews and testimonials from readers can be powerful endorsements of your expertise. Encourage readers to leave reviews on platforms like Amazon and Goodreads, and to share their thoughts on social media. Highlight these testimonials in your marketing materials, on your website and in proposals to prospective clients.

Build an online community

Create an online community around your book and its themes. This could be a forum on your website, a LinkedIn group or a Facebook page. Use this space to foster discussions, share resources and connect with your readers on a deeper level.

An engaged community not only supports your book's message but also provides valuable feedback and ideas for future projects. It is also a pool of hot prospects who already feel they know you and are eager to buy your services.

Speaking engagements and keynotes

Leverage your authority as a published author to secure speaking engagements, keynotes and panel participation at industry conferences, corporate events and workshops. These platforms allow you to reach a broader audience, share your expertise, and drive interest in your book and related offerings. Speaking engagements can also lead to media exposure, further amplifying your impact.

Ongoing learning and adaptation

To scale your impact effectively, commit to ongoing learning and adaptation. Stay in the know about the latest trends and challenges in your field and be open to evolving your message and offerings accordingly.

It is not a huge deal to update your manuscript and publish an updated version. This not only keeps your brand relevant but also ensures that you continue to provide value to your audience and remain at the forefront of your industry.

Leveraging media and public relations

A strategic public relations campaign can elevate your profile and extend your reach beyond your existing network. Pitch story ideas related to your book's theme to relevant media outlets, offer yourself as an expert for interviews and contribute op-eds or articles to industry publications. Media exposure can significantly boost your credibility and attract audiences.

A book is a multifaceted tool that, when leveraged correctly, can significantly amplify your business growth and brand development. By establishing your authority, integrating your book into your marketing strategy, using it as a lead generation tool and exploring new opportunities for training and collaboration, you can maximise the return on your investment in writing and publishing your book.

Remember, the journey doesn't end with publication, it's just the beginning of leveraging your book to achieve greater success. By adopting these strategies, you can extend the reach of your message, create opportunities for growth and continue to build your authority and influence in your field. Your book is just the beginning – your potential for impact is limitless.

> *Very few people make it all the way through the writing, publishing and marketing process. This includes your competitors. By creating a book and using it as the cornerstone of your lead generation and marketing efforts, you will leave your competitors on the horizon and position yourself as the most sought-after person in your field.*

TARRYN REEVES

AUTHOR, SPEAKER AND PUBLISHER

CONCLUSION

CHAPTER 28

THE AUTOMATIC AUTHORITY BOOK WRITING CHALLENGE
Write, Publish, and Become a Bestselling Author in the Next Six Months

Now I know this book is all about writing yours within 28 days, but I like a challenge and I hope you do, too. I want to challenge you to **write and publish** your book within six months of starting the process.

You've wasted enough time on outdated marketing techniques and playing at a lower level than you know you are meant to do. If you stick to this plan, you can transform your life and business for the better within the next six months.

Let's do it!

Weeks 1–2: Ideation and planning

- **Define your book's purpose:** Clarify what you want to achieve with your book and the value it will provide to your readers.

- **Conduct market research:** Identify your target audience, its needs and how your book will meet those needs.

- **Choose your topic:** Select a topic that aligns with your expertise, audience interest and market demand.

- **Outline your book:** Create a detailed chapter outline, breaking down each chapter into sections and key points.

- **Choose your publishing route:** Decide between self-publishing, hybrid publishing or traditional publishing based on your goals, and then prepare your submission and engage a hybrid publisher or select your publishing platform set-up.

Weeks 3–7: Writing phase

- **Establish a daily writing habit:** Determine your daily word count target and set aside dedicated writing time each day.
- **Start writing:** Begin with the chapters or sections you feel most comfortable with to gain momentum.
- **Stay on track:** Monitor your progress regularly and adjust your schedule as needed to meet your writing goals.

Weeks 8–10: First round of edits

- **Self-edit:** Review your manuscript for content clarity, coherence and consistency. Make necessary revisions to improve the flow and structure.
- **Beta readers:** Share your draft with a select group of beta readers for feedback on content, readability and engagement.

Weeks 11–13: Professional editing

- **Hire a professional editor:** Engage a professional editor to refine your manuscript, focusing on developmental editing and copy editing.
- **Incorporate feedback:** Review the edited manuscript and make final adjustments based on the editor's recommendations.

Weeks 14–16: Design and formatting

- **Cover design:** Work with a designer to create a professional and compelling cover.
- **Interior layout:** Have your manuscript professionally formatted for print and digital formats.
- **Final proofread:** Conduct a final proofread to catch any lingering errors.

Weeks 17–20: Prepare for launch

- **Set up pre-orders:** If self-publishing, set up pre-orders on platforms like Amazon.
- **Plan your launch strategy:** Outline your launch plan, including marketing efforts, launch team coordination and event planning.

Weeks 20–24: Launch

- **Execute your launch plan:** Implement your marketing and promotional strategies to generate buzz and drive initial sales.
- **Host your launch event:** Celebrate your book's release with a launch event, either virtual or in person, to thank your supporters and promote your book.

Post-launch – scaling your impact

- **Monitor and adjust marketing efforts:** Keep track of your book's performance and adjust marketing strategies as needed.
- **Leverage your book for growth:** Use your book as a tool for developing business, networking and establishing yourself as an authority in your field.

Completing the Automatic Authority Book Writing Challenge is a testament to your commitment, discipline and passion for sharing your knowledge and expertise. By following this step-by-step action plan, you've not only achieved the remarkable feat of publishing a book, but you have also set the stage for greater influence, authority and success in your business endeavours.

Remember, the journey doesn't end here. Your book is a living asset that will continue to open doors, create opportunities and have an impact on lives.

To help you implement this chapter I have included an additional book bonus called the 28-Day Book Challenge Writing Guide. To access this bonus resource, scan the QR code below.

"

It always seems impossible until it's done.

NELSON MANDELA

ANTI-APARTHEID ACTIVIST AND POLITICIAN

YOUR NEXT STEPS

We are nearing the end of my book, and I wholeheartedly hope that you have gained a lot from choosing to spend your time reading it.

Here's what we covered:

In the first few chapters, we took a look at why a book is the best method to simplify your marketing, grow your authority and turn cold leads into pre-qualified, ready-to-buy prospects for your next level offers.

This was followed by a journey to discover who it is you are actually writing your book for and the exact blueprint you need to write a book that creates loyal fans ready to buy your product and vision.

Next, we looked at what it takes to set yourself up for success including choosing your topic, how to work smarter and what it takes to write a bestselling book.

The chapters that followed showed you exactly, piece by piece, how to write your book. And even better, how to write your book within 28 days without having to hit pause on your lifestyle.

We then took an in-depth look at the art of storytelling, followed by a brief foray into the publishing world and how to launch and market your book for success.

To round it all off, I threw down a challenge to you – to write and publish your book within 90 days.

But it's not over yet.

I couldn't help but throw in a few bonus chapters that looked at some useful tools to help keep you accountable to your goal of getting shit done, and a discussion of how to get out of your own way.

And that, my friend, brings us to the final piece, which is for you to take action, if you haven't already.

Kiss your excuses goodbye and just WRITE.

AN INVITATION

I've included several resources throughout the book and given you the exact information you will need to get your book written in 28 days or less. If you follow what I have shared with you, then you will end up with a book that will be an asset for your business for years.

But I don't want our time together to end here. I want to provide as much value to you as possible, for whatever stage of the journey you are on, as and when you need it. So, with that in mind, I am going to make you several offers.

Join our Mastermind

Join our exclusive Mastermind designed for ambitious authors who dream of writing, publishing and marketing a bestselling book that not only cements their status as authorities in their field, but also turns readers into loyal fans eager to part with their money and buy their next level offerings.

This Mastermind is your golden ticket to navigating the complex journey of creating a book with ease and confidence. You'll gain access to a wealth of professional support, from crafting compelling content that resonates with your target audience to implementing cutting-edge marketing strategies that amplify your reach and impact.

Our goal is not just to help you write and publish a book, but to ensure it's a sensational success that enhances your professional stature, expands your influence and creates a loyal fan base ready to engage with your endeavours.

If you're ready to take your expertise to the next level and transform your insights into a powerful legacy, the Automatic Authority Business School is where your bestselling author journey begins.

Join the Mastermind by scanning the QR code below:

Experience one of our three levels of intimate partnership experiences

The Triple-A Experience

Embark on an intimate one-to-one, three-stage partnership journey with us to transform your idea into a successfully launched non-fiction book in 180 days or less – guaranteed. Our comprehensive support ensures that you:

- Proudly author a high-quality non-fiction book, doubling as an impeccable marketing asset for your business.
- Achieve #1 Amazon Bestselling Author status in at least three categories on launch day.
- Secure at least 200 book sales within the first 30 days post-launch.
- Garner at least 50 genuine Amazon book reviews within the first 30 days of your book's release.

The Triple-A VIP Experience

Elevate your book's success and your professional standing with the Triple-A VIP Experience. This elite service not only guarantees the triumph of your publication but also establishes you as a distinguished authority in your field. Benefit from:

- Enhanced visibility through our dedicated PR and media efforts.
- Expanded distribution of your book, both online and in physical stores, for maximum reach and impact.
- A seamless journey to becoming a globally recognised brand and authority.

The Triple-A 'WOW' Experience

Transform your professional identity with the Triple-A 'WOW' Experience, where becoming a respected author is just the beginning. Ascend to the heights of influence as a TEDx speaker, a sought-after TV personality and a symbol of unmatched credibility. This transformative package offers:

- An opportunity to have a profound and inspirational impact on a global audience.
- The platform to share your insights and effect change on a monumental scale.
- A complete metamorphosis of your professional identity, ensuring you are celebrated as an icon of authority and influence.

Each experience is designed to cater to your unique ambitions, ensuring not just the success of your book, but also a significant elevation of your professional profile.

If you wish to learn more about working with my team and myself on a one-to-one basis, scan the QR code below:

And if you are choosing not to join my team and me in any of the above, that's also okay. No judgement here. I know that what I have provided you will enable you to create an amazing book, and I will be cheering you on from the sidelines.

And when you complete your book and send it forth into the world, please send me a signed copy. I would be proud to showcase you and your brilliance.

You've got this.

Now get writing.

Love,

Tarryn

BONUS CONTENT

BONUS CHAPTER 1

NAILING YOUR PROFESSIONAL BIOGRAPHY

You will want to include your professional biography at the end of your book so people can learn more about you and understand that you are the go-to expert on your chosen topic. Even though they would have just read your amazing book, this part helps to solidify your authority on the subject.

When writing your professional biography, the first step is to choose the right format. Traditionally, people have gone for a chronological approach which details work or business history and education in chronological order. Alternatively, you can go for a more skills-based approach, which will highlight your key skills and accomplishments.

My favourite format is the simple, conversational one, so that is what I am going to cover here.

Start by stating who you are, what you do, who you do it for and the results people can expect from working with you or from buying your product.

You can then include a paragraph that covers your achievements, awards, media appearances and skill set.

The third and final paragraph is designed to share something personal, such as where you live, who you live with and what you do in your spare time.

You will then include contact details and social links beneath.

Remember that this is not actually about you. Your readers are searching for something for themselves. Your biography needs to be short but impactful and help your readers clearly see that you are the expert and the right person to support them with what they are seeking.

Check out my biography at the end of this book for inspiration.

I have also included The Professional Author Biography Worksheet below to help you draft a professional author biography. I dare you to tell us how amazing you are. Do it!

"

The more you praise and celebrate your life, the more there is in life to celebrate.

OPRAH WINFREY

AMERICAN TALK SHOW HOST, TELEVISION PRODUCER,
ACTOR, AUTHOR AND MEDIA PROPRIETOR

The Professional Author Biography Worksheet

Objective: To draft a professional author biography.

1. Who is your ideal client?
2. What results do your clients get from working with you or buying your products?
3. Complete the sentence below:
   (Your full name) is the (your job title) of (your company name). He/She/They works with (your ideal client) to (pain point identified) so that they can (how the client can move from point A to point B with your support).
4. List your achievements, awards, media appearances and expertise.
5. What personal touch would you like to include in the final paragraph?
6. What contact details and social links would you like to include?
7. Which professional photo would you like to use to accompany your biography?

You can do this exercise on a piece of paper, or if you'd like to download a digital version of this worksheet, scan the QR code below:

BONUS CHAPTER 2

ACE IT WITH ACCOUNTABILITY

In the solitary journey of writing, where the only company is the blinking cursor on a blank page, the importance of an accountability partner cannot be overstated. As the days turn into weeks and the weeks into months, the initial enthusiasm that fuelled your creative spark may begin to wane.

This is where the accountability partner steps in, not merely as a writing companion but as a dedicated ally in your literary conquest.

The solitude of the writer

Writing is often a solitary pursuit (unless you take advantage of our epic co-writing sessions inside the Automatic Authority community. See the QR code at the end of this chapter). Armed with nothing but your thoughts and a keyboard, you hope to delve into the recesses of your imagination to weave wisdom, share lessons and craft narratives.

However, this isolation can become a double-edged sword. While it allows for deep introspection and undisturbed creativity, it also opens the door for procrastination and self-doubt. Getting up and down 500 times during your writing session to 'just take care of something' will not get your book written. I get it – I really do. I can't sit still to save my life, but it's something you must practise if you want to finish your manuscript.

Enter the accountability partner

Think of an accountability partner like the Robin to your Batman, the Bonnie to your Clyde, or my personal favourite, the Hermione to your Ron (J.K. Rowling, you are amazing).

An accountability partner is more than just someone to share progress updates with. Your partner is a lifeline, a source of motivation and a gentle but firm push when needed. This person is someone who understands the struggles and triumphs of the writing process intimately, having probably experienced them first-hand.

The power of commitment

When you have an accountability partner, you're not just committed to yourself and your project, you are now part of a team. This commitment goes beyond personal discipline, it becomes a shared responsibility.

The awareness that someone is counting on you, someone is invested in your success, transforms the act of writing from an individual endeavour to a collaborative effort. When you're committed to another person to get something done, and you know that person is going to hold you accountable, you are much less likely to procrastinate.

Setting goals and deadlines

One primary function of an accountability partner is to help set realistic goals and deadlines. With the looming presence of a writing companion, the abstract concept of 'someday finishing the book' instead becomes a tangible timeline. Whether it's a weekly word count, a chapter draft by a certain date or a regular check-in, these milestones provide structure to the often chaotic world of writing and entrepreneurship.

Motivation in moments of despair

Writing is not always smooth sailing. There are moments of self-doubt, writer's block and existential crises. During these times, the accountability partner becomes a beacon of encouragement. Beyond the technical aspects of writing, the partner is there to remind you of the importance of your story, the uniqueness of your voice and the significance of your message.

Celebrating success together

Completing a book is a monumental achievement, and sharing that success with someone who has been with you every step of the way adds a layer of joy and fulfilment. Your victories become shared victories and the sense of accomplishment is magnified.

Choosing your accountability partner wisely

Not all partnerships are created equal. Choosing an accountability partner who understands your writing style, shares your commitment and who can provide constructive feedback is crucial. It's probably a good idea that you share some similar interests, too. You don't want a writing partner who grates on your nerves.

Mutual respect and understanding are the foundations of a successful writing partnership.

In the quest to transform ideas into words and words into a narrative, an accountability partner is the unsung hero, the silent force that nudges you forward when the weight of the blank page seems impossible. Embrace the power of partnership, for in the shared journey lies the strength to turn your writing dreams into a tangible reality.

Get your accountability partner today

Inside the Automatic Authority community you're among like-minded, brilliant people (yourself included). I also know that the journey of writing your book can sometimes feel lonely, which is why I want to make it easy for you to find an accountability partner.

Having an accountability partner can dramatically increase the possibility of successfully getting your book written, so don't dilly-dally in finding your accountability partner or partners. You've got money to make!

The trick here is to stay consistent and meet regularly. The main purpose of your meetings is to review goals, identify where you are in your writing journey, and establish the next step you need to take to get one step closer to having your book written.

To find an accountability partner, join the Automatic Authority community using the QR code below:

I have also put together a handy checklist and writing buddy meeting agenda to help you get started.

"

Accountability is the glue that ties commitment to the result.

BOB PROCTOR

AUTHOR AND LECTURER

Writing Buddy Checklist

Objective: To ensure both you and your writing partner stay aligned with your goals.

- Find a writing buddy.
- Agree on a weekly meeting day and time.
- Add the meetings to your calendar.
- Set up your meeting link.
- Agree on how you will contact each other in the event of last-minute changes, meaning you can't make the meeting.
- Allow an extra 15 minutes on your first meeting to get to know each other better. I suggest discussing how you would like to receive feedback and if you would like there to be a consequence if you don't complete your action items from the previous meeting.

If you would like to download a fillable PDF version of this checklist, scan the QR code below:

Writing Buddy Meeting Agenda

Day: _____

Time: _____

1. What next step did you commit to taking from our meeting last week?

_____

_____

_____

_____

_____

2. Did you get it done?

   ☐ Yes
   ☐ No
   ☐ Some of it

3. If partially or not, what challenges did you experience?

_____

_____

_____

4. How can you overcome these challenges?

_____

_____

_____

_____

_____

5. What is the next step you will commit to take this week that will
    move you closer to getting your book written?

_____

_____

_____

_____

_____

You can do this exercise on a piece of paper, or if you'd like to download
a digital version of this worksheet, scan the QR code below:

BONUS CHAPTER 3

OVERCOMING OBSTACLES

Many things can get in the way of writing. Sometimes it's hard to find the motivation to sit down and start putting words on paper or screen, while at other times we get stuck trying to come up with a good idea. And sometimes, the biggest challenge is just getting through the final draft. Obstacles are an inevitable part of the process.

In this chapter, we will discuss some of the most common obstacles writers face and how to overcome them.

Writer's block: the uninvited guest

Ah, the infamous writer's block – the bane of every wordsmith's existence. Picture this: you're staring at a blank page and it's almost mocking you with its emptiness, or the cursor blinks, seemingly in rhythm with your mounting frustration. Ideas? They're playing a game of hide-and-seek, and right now, they're winning.

It's like standing at the edge of a vast, unexplored landscape, armed with only a pen and a mind that's seemingly empty. The blank page, once a canvas for creativity, now feels like a daunting abyss. It's not just a lack of inspiration, it's a full-on blockade, a mental traffic jam that leaves you stuck in a sea of uncharted thoughts.

And let's talk about those elusive ideas. They're like mischievous sprites, flitting in and out of your consciousness and teasing you with their presence before slipping away like smoke. You reach out to grab one. Poof! It's gone! You are left with nothing but the echo of what could have been a brilliant concept.

But here's the thing about writer's block – it's a rite of passage for wordsmiths. It's that challenging level in the game of creativity – the boss battle – that separates the novices from the seasoned pros. Because in that moment of staring at the blank page, you're not just facing a lack of ideas, you're facing yourself – your doubts, your insecurities and that nagging voice whispering, 'What if you can't do this?'

Yet, every writer has an arsenal against this formidable foe. Some swear by the power of a change of scenery – a coffee shop, a park, anywhere that isn't the oppressive stare of the blank page. Others find solace in the rhythmic clacking of keys, the physical act of typing somehow coaxing those ideas out of hiding.

And then there are those who embrace the chaos. They scribble, they doodle, they throw words on to the page like paint on a canvas. Because sometimes, the best way to conquer the blank page is not with a carefully crafted strategy, but with a reckless abandonment of perfection.

Embrace the concept of what I call the 'first bad draft'. Give yourself permission to write what your inner critic undoubtedly labels as shitty writing. The important thing is to get words on paper. Set small, achievable goals and don't be afraid to write 'badly'. You can always edit and revise later.

So, the next time you find yourself locked in a battle with writer's block, remember this – you're not alone. Every author has stood where you are, from the humble beginner to the seasoned veteran. The blank page is just a canvas, and the beauty of creation lies in the chaos that precedes it.

Embrace the challenge, let the ideas dance in and out and you'll have conquered the blank page before you know it.

Perfectionism: the silent saboteur

The pursuit of perfection is a bit like chasing a mirage in the desert – it seems within reach but the closer you get the more it slips away. As writers, we often find ourselves tangled in the web of perfectionism, where every word needs to be flawless, every sentence a masterpiece.

One minute you're in the zone and the next you're sitting in front of your computer, fingers poised over the keyboard as a page stares back at you like a judgemental critic. You want your writing to be impeccable, a literary marvel that stands the test of time. The only problem is that you're stuck in the quest for unattainable perfection. It's a bit like trying to sprint through quicksand – lots of effort but not much progress.

Perfectionism can be a demanding companion, whispering in your ear that your work is never good enough (I swear that for me it's like another personality). It's the nagging voice that makes you second-guess every word, every comma and every piece of wisdom you want to share. You find yourself editing and re-editing, endlessly tweaking and adjusting, but the finish line seems to recede with each change. It's a frustrating loop that can turn the joy of writing into a tedious chore.

In the grand scheme of things, imperfections are the spice of life and the same holds true for writing. The quirks and idiosyncrasies of a piece give it character and authenticity. It's the raw, unpolished edges that make a story relatable and which allow you to create relationships with your dream clients from the pages of your book without ever having to hop on another Zoom call.

Perfection might be a tempting goal but it's an illusion that can keep us from sharing our stories with the world and moving our businesses forward.

Imagine if J.K. Rowling had agonised over making every sentence in Harry Potter flawless – where would the magic be in that? Imagine if Alex Hormozi worried that the drawings in his books were too childish.

Sometimes it's the messy imperfection that paves the way for greatness.

Writing is a journey, not a destination, and getting lost in the pursuit of perfection can mean missing out on the scenery along the way.

So, let's cut ourselves some slack. Embrace the beauty in imperfection, relish the spontaneity of a first draft, and remember that the real joy of writing comes from the process and not the elusive goal of perfection. After all, the world needs your story, your work, with all its quirks and imperfections, far more than it needs another flawless manuscript gathering dust on a forgotten shelf.

Time management: juggling business, life and writing

You're busy. I get it. Me, too. Everyone is. Diving into the world of writing while juggling the myriad responsibilities life throws at you can feel a bit like trying to walk a tightrope while throwing and catching flaming torches. It's this delicate dance between writing the book that will change your life and the reality of a bustling, busy existence. It's no easy feat but it absolutely can, and must, be done.

Often, you will have just sat down, had a brainstorming session for the next chapter and been ready to pound it out, and then reality suddenly taps you on the shoulder, reminding you of that looming deadline of client work, the mountain of laundry that refuses to wash itself, and the dinner you promised your family. Suddenly, your writing takes a backseat to the daily grind and more 'urgent' business priorities.

But here's the thing – navigating the choppy waters of everyday responsibilities and the need to write your book is not an either-or scenario. It's a delicate art of harmonising the two. You learn to steal moments, scribbling down ideas on the back of grocery lists, weaving chapters in your mind during the school run, and maybe even sacrificing a bit of sleep in the name of crafting the perfect sentence.

It's a journey of learning to embrace the ebb and flow of creativity amid the chaos of life. Some days, you'll feel like you're conquering the literary world, typing away at your manuscript with the finesse of a maestro. On other days, the laundry, the emails and the demands of the world might seem like an insurmountable mountain casting a shadow over your desk.

Yet, amid the chaos, there's a certain magic in finding stolen moments to nurture your passion. It's there in those furtive glances at your notebook while making dinner, the quiet typing in the late hours of the night, and the joyous celebration of finishing a chapter, even if it meant sacrificing another episode of your favourite TV show (I'm watching Lucifer at the moment), and it's that magic that keeps you going.

So, while balancing writing with the rest of life's responsibilities may be a challenge, it's a challenge worth embracing. It's about understanding that the journey to getting your book done is as much about the process as it is about the destination. After all, the best work often emerges from the intricate tapestry of our daily lives, woven together with threads of responsibility, passion and a dash of daring to dream.

Establish a writing routine that works for you, and imagine having a writing routine that's as comfy as your favourite hoodie. It could be the crack of dawn when the world is still wrapped in a cosy blanket of quiet, or maybe it's the deep embrace of the night when the stars are your only companions, and the house is finally quiet. Heck, it might even be those sacred lunch breaks between client sessions, when you find a chance to pen down your thoughts.

Consistency is also key. It's like the secret sauce that makes your writing journey as smooth as a jazz melody (anyone else like a bit of jazz?). Break down those writing goals into bite-sized, manageable tasks. Don't see it as a mountain but as a bunch of easily conquerable hills. Much less daunting, right?

First, there's routine, then there's consistency and now comes time management. Let's be the superheroes of our schedules. Prioritise like you're picking flavours at an ice cream parlour. What do you want on top? Your time is precious, so spend it on the tasks that truly matter. It's not just about writing. It's about making your minutes count. Protect your writing time like you would a booked appointment with your highest-paying client, because your book will ultimately result in multiple high-paying clients.

Now, here's the plot twist. Share your writing aspirations with those around you. Your family, friends, and even your pet iguana – let them in on the literary adventure. Trust me, having a support system is like having a squad of cheerleaders. They'll help you through those moments of writer's block and celebrate your victories, big or small.

So, there you have it – the recipe for a writing routine that's as unique as your fingerprint. It's about finding your golden hour, slicing your goals into manageable bits, mastering the art of juggling time and having your personal fan club to cheer you on. Happy writing!

Lack of motivation: navigating the doldrums

Writing a book is like a marathon, a roller-coaster of emotions, and there are bound to be moments when your motivation takes a nosedive. But fear not; there are some nifty tricks to reignite that fiery passion for your project and keep those creative juices flowing.

First things first, let's talk goals. Break down your mammoth of a project into bite-sized, manageable targets. Setting short-term milestones is like giving yourself little checkpoints to celebrate along the way. Completing a chapter, hitting a word count goal or even just conquering a particularly tricky reword of your unique method are all victories worth celebrating. It's like fuel for your writer's soul.

Don't skimp on the mini parties for yourself. Treat yourself to a favourite snack, indulge in a guilty pleasure TV show or take a victory lap around your living room. Do, whatever makes you happy and marks the occasion. Trust me, these small celebrations can be the lifebuoy that keeps you afloat when motivation is scarcer than toilet paper in a pandemic.

And if you're the type of person who likes people, writing doesn't have to be a solitary journey. Joining a writing group or finding a fellow scribbler to be your accountability partner can be a game-changer (refer back to Bonus Chapter 2 if you have yet to take action on this one – tut tut).

Having someone to share your triumphs and struggles with not only provides a fresh perspective but also serves as a source of motivation. It's like having a personal cheerleader, and who doesn't love a good cheer?

Sometimes, a change of scenery is all you need to shake things up. If your writing space has started to feel like a creative black hole, venture into the great unknown. Try a new cafe, a library or even a park bench. The world is your writing oyster, my friend.

And if you're really feeling adventurous, dive into some writing exercises. They're like the jumping jacks for your brain. They can kick-start your creativity and help you see your project from a different angle, adding a pinch of spice to your writing routine – a little zest to keep things interesting.

So there you have it – a toolkit for keeping the writing flame burning. Embrace the ups and downs, celebrate the victories and, most importantly, enjoy the ride.

Self-doubt: the inner critic

Every writer has moments where doubt creeps in like an uninvited guest at a party. You start to question if your words are worthy, if your story has the spark it needs or if you're just playing pretend.

But here's the thing: self-doubt is not some rare creature that visits only you. It's the sidekick to creativity – nay, to the human experience. We've all been there, staring at a blank page, wondering if the words we're about to scrawl on to it will ever be worth anyone's time.

In those moments, channelling your inner superhero and challenging those negative thoughts is crucial. Picture doubt as a villain, and you, with your superpower of words, poised to defeat it.

Instead of dwelling on what might go wrong, focus on your strengths. Remind yourself of those moments when your work changed someone's life, or when you knew in your bones that this is the work you came here to do. Celebrate the victories no matter how small. You've got a super-power and it's time to unleash it. Nobody can do what you can do in the unique way that you do it. Nobody.

Now, there's a secret weapon against the doubting demons – a community of fellow entrepreneurial writers (I know … here I go again, but it's obviously important if I keep harping on about it). These are the comrades who've fought similar battles and who understand the struggles and triumphs of crafting a book designed to act as a simplified marketing strategy that floods pipelines with leads.

Surround yourself with these allies. Share your fears, your victories and your wild ideas. Their encouragement is like a power-up, boosting your morale and reminding you that you're not alone in this creative chaos.

And let's not forget writing is a craft not a one-time magic trick. It's a skill that gets sharper with every word you write. Think of it like learning to play an instrument. At first, your notes might be a bit off, but with practice you create symphonies. It's also a skill you can take forward into all aspects of your business, from social media to sales calls. After all, storytelling sells.

So, don't be too hard on yourself. Everyone starts somewhere, even the literary and entrepreneurial giants we admire. They, too, had to (and

I can guarantee still do) navigate the maze of self-doubt and emerge victorious.

In the grand tapestry of storytelling and entrepreneurship, doubt is just a thread and not the whole picture. Embrace it as part of the creative process but don't let it steal the spotlight. You're the author of your narrative. Every word you write or speak is a brushstroke on the canvas of your success. Wield that pen or keyboard with confidence, and remember the world is waiting to read what you have to say.

Fear of failure: embracing the unknown

Fear of failure can be paralysing, preventing us from taking risks or pursuing ambitious projects. This is totally understandable. The entrepreneurial and the writing journey is like a roller-coaster through the unknown, and the fear of failure is that nagging voice that says, 'Hey, what if this doesn't work out?'

Let me remind you of something you already know – embracing uncertainty is where the magic happens. That fear you're feeling? It's just a sign that you're on to something big, something that could redefine your life in all the best ways.

Failure? Well, it's not the monster under your desk. It's more like a wonky stepping stone on the path to success. Every one of us has stumbled over a challenge or two. It's practically a rite of passage. So, instead of seeing failure as the big bad wolf, consider it your wise mentor nudging you towards growth.

And hey, let's talk about the process. We're all guilty of fixating on the outcome, right? Will this book be a bestseller? (It will be if you work with us, we guarantee it.) Will it win awards? But what about the process itself? The messy drafts, the scribbled notes, the late-night revelations? Don't panic, friend, that's where the real magic is.

Writing is a journey, not just a destination. Each hiccup, each obstacle is a chance to flex those creative muscles and learn more about yourself and just how powerful your work really is. Think of writing as doing literary push-ups. Sure, it might sting a bit, but oh, the strength you gain from it!

So next time that fear of failure starts doing the cha-cha in your mind, give it a little nod, maybe a high-five and then show it the door. Embrace the uncertainty, my friend. Your next adventure awaits and it's going to be one heck of a ride.

> ## "
>
> *Only crazy people are entrepreneurs. It's like getting punched in the face again and again, yet we keep coming back for more.*

TARRYN REEVES (THAT'S ME!)

AUTHOR, PUBLISHER AND SPEAKER

ACKNOWLEDGEMENTS

As with everything in life, it takes several people to achieve something, anything really. Behind every successful endeavour is a team of support people giving what they can to support their person on a mission.

First, I want to thank my coach Dimitri Ross. You are hands down the best business coach I have had. Without you, and your loving but savage accountability, this book would not have seen the light of day for many more years. Thank you.

To my children, Autumn and Harvey. Thank you for being semi-patient while Mumma had to work. You inspire and teach me something every day. Thank you for being my greatest teachers and being the constant reminders of why I do what I do. You're my 'why' when the going gets tough.

I would not be where I am without my incredible team. Each and every one of you is so valued and the company is as great as it is because you are a part of it. Thank you for your amazing skill sets, your time, your expertise, for listening to my crazy ideas and for being patient when I'm Mumming. I love you all.

Thank you to all my clients past, current and future. Thank you for trusting my team and me with your work. It is an honour to walk beside you as you bring your ideas into the world. I get the greatest joy from our co-creative journey. This isn't just business for me, it's my purpose. You help me fulfil that every time you say yes to working with me. Thank you.

Finally, I want to thank you, the person reading this book. Thank you for acting on your curiosity that led you to pick it up in the first place. Thank you for spending your precious time with me as you journeyed through these pages. And thank you for being brave enough to take action and bring your book to life. The world needs you and your wisdom.

ABOUT THE AUTHOR

Tarryn Reeves is the founder of Automatic Authority Publishing & Press House. She is an author on multiple international bestselling lists (including *USA Today*), a book coach, publisher, freelance writer, ghostwriter and speaker whose work has been featured in Forbes, *Newsweek*, the *Los Angeles Times*, World News Network, Thrive Global and more.

Tarryn and her team work together with high-level entrepreneurs to create bestselling books that act as marketing tools and authority builders, to grow businesses and create ripple effects with an impact across the globe.

Tarryn lives in Australia with her children, Autumn and Harvey. When she isn't creating bestsellers, she can be found reading, adventuring in nature or relaxing with a cup of tea.

www.tarrynreeves.com

www.automaticauthority.com